THE CHRISTIAN LIFE
IN THE
MIDDLE AGES
AND OTHER ESSAYS

THE CHRISTIAN LIFE IN THE MIDDLE AGES

AND OTHER ESSAYS

By

SIR MAURICE POWICKE

OXFORD
AT THE CLARENDON PRESS

Oxford University Press, Great Clarendon Street, Oxford OX2 6DP
Oxford New York
Athens Auckland Bangkok Bogota Bombay
Buenos Aires Calcutta Cape Town Dar es Salaam
Delhi Florence Hong Kong Istanbul Karachi
Kuala Lumpur Madras Madrid Melbourne
Mexico City Nairobi Paris Singapore
Taipei Tokyo Toronto
and associated companies in
Berlin Ibadan

Published in the United States by
Oxford University Press Inc., New York

First published by Oxford University Press 1935
Reprinted 1966, 1968
Special edition for Sandpiper Books Ltd., 1997

British Library Cataloguing in Publication Data
Data available

Library of Congress Cataloging in Publication Data

ISBN 0-19-821460-X

5 7 9 10 8 6 4

Printed in Great Britain by
Bookcraft Ltd
Midsomer Norton, Somerset

PREFACE

THE following papers were written at different times and for various occasions. The story of the countess Loretta involved some minute investigation, and the lecture on Stephen Langton contains unpublished material which I owe to the kindness of a friend, but the papers, regarded as a whole, are the outcome neither of elaborate research nor, as learned men use the phrase, of very wide reading. Yet I hope that they are the result of something more than casual reflection. I have put them together—not entirely on my own initiative—because they seem to have something in common which may justify their appearance in a more accessible form. With more or less intensity and deliberation, they are attempts to illustrate problems in the life of the Christian Church which have never been so urgent as they were in the long period of European history when many social traditions, of varying degrees of crudity or sophistication, were gradually mingled together. The stress and strain which resulted from this slow formation of western civilization can be seen throughout modern history, in the conflict between liberty and order, and in the endless warfare between the desire for self-expression and the impulse to self-surrender. But I have been much more concerned to dwell upon these issues as an expression of medieval life than to analyse the 'legacy' of the Middle Ages. To regard them as important only because of the results which we deduce from them, to arrange the past neatly as a process in which the most significant things are those which are most easily appropriated by the present, is to do disservice to history. If the study of the past is to enlarge experience, it must take account of the 'spiritual presences of absent things'. Still less should we see in the past a struggle between clearly defined good and evil, in which the good survives; and even if we convince ourselves that the experiences which painfully emerged from medieval society—the national state, 'evangelical' religion, the scientific mind—are permanently good, the fulfilment of purpose working in the medieval world, we who have entered into them cannot trace our spiritual ancestry. 'Ideals', Croce has said, 'may well be theoretically divided into good and bad, into superior and inferior, but men—and the actual battle is one of men against men—cannot be thus divided and set off against one another, and each one of them contains within himself in varying degree the true and the false, the high and the low, spirit and matter.'

Six of the eight papers in this volume have been printed before. Apart from some corrections, omissions, and minor changes, they are reprinted as they appeared. Most of the footnotes have been deleted. I have to thank the editors of *History*, the *Bulletin of the John Rylands Library*, and *Theology*, the Council of the Royal Historical Society, and the editors of the *Historical Essays in Honour of James Tait* for permission to reprint the five papers which first appeared under their auspices. The paper on 'Dante and the Crusade' and the lecture on medieval education have not previously been printed.

F. M. P.

Oriel College, Oxford.

CONTENTS

BIBLIOGRAPHICAL NOTE

'The Christian Life', in *The Legacy of the Middle Ages* (Oxford, 1926).

'Pope Boniface VIII', in *History* (March 1934).

'Some Problems in the History of the Medieval University', in *Transactions of the Royal Historical Society* (1934).

'Gerald of Wales', in *The Bulletin of the John Rylands Library* (July 1928).

'Stephen Langton', in *Theology* (August 1928).

'Loretta, Countess of Leicester', in *Historical Essays in Honour of James Tait* (Manchester, 1933).

I

THE CHRISTIAN LIFE IN THE MIDDLE AGES

THE legacy of medieval Christianity to later ages was the problem of authority. Christians, it is unnecessary to add, did not create the problem, which is involved in the art of conscious living, but they revealed it in all the bewildering amplitude of the conflict between order and freedom, between obedience to Christ and submission to His Church. They have never been proud of it, for it has been to them a tiresome perplexity, an unmanageable side-issue in a labour vastly more important. Organized Christianity came into existence, and exists, to preserve a treasure, a command to be executed, a promise to be repeated, a mission to be fulfilled. This treasure belongs to past, present, and future; it is potential, yet active; an object of contemplation, yet the inspiration of right conduct. An unfathomable mystery, it must be related to all knowledge. And in their endeavours to guard and transmit their trust, its guardians have raised the most perplexing issues. They have caused endless destruction of life in the name of universal peace. They have built up the most realistic of political systems in the effort to establish a kingdom not of this world. In the exploration of the recesses of the soul, they have developed the arts and sciences, and constructed theories of the universe. And, in their desire to satisfy the deepest needs of mankind, they have raised up against themselves the visions, prophecies, and extravagances of excitable and obstinate men, and the dislike of many sensible men.

The treasure which has caused all this activity was cast into the world with a few simple sentences. 'Thou shalt love the Lord thy God and thy neighbour as thyself. What shall it profit a man if he shall gain the whole world and lose his own soul?' And again, 'God so loved the world that he gave his only begotten Son, that whosoever believeth in Him should not perish but have everlasting life. No one cometh to the Father, save by Me. Take, eat; this is my body.' And again, 'Go and preach the Kingdom of God.

Feed my sheep. Thou art Peter, and upon this rock will I build my Church. Peace I leave with you, my peace I give unto you. I have come not to bring peace, but a sword.'

I

Only those who accept the dogma of the divinity of Christ as the central fact in a long process of divine revelation can escape bewilderment in the contemplation of the spread of Christianity, which has been so unlike other religions in its claim to penetrate and control the whole of life. The historian, who must discard dogmas, betrays his bewilderment at every step. He tends to explain the history of the Church by explaining it away. The absorption of Greek thought and the penetration of the traditions of Rome by the new life and teaching are regarded as causes rather than as effects of their success. The Word was not as leaven; it was an artificial result of the strange ferment of religious excitement, superstitions, philosophical mysticism, desperate aspirations which stirred among the peoples of the Levant. Even if the Gospel narratives are accepted as generally true, reason and imagination combine in our days to reject the claims of any body of men, living a fragile life in a world which is but a speck in an infinite universe, to interpret with infallible accuracy the significance of the life of Christ, both for every human soul and in the whole process of nature. Whatever welcome Christ might receive to-day it is inconceivable that the later history of his followers could in the remotest degree resemble the history of the Christian Church.

We have not to inquire whether, in the conditions of life which prevailed during the early centuries, the spread of Christianity was as remarkable as it would be to-day. Probably we under-estimate the extent to which the Gospel appealed then to the trained intellect, just as we over-estimate the extent to which modern science has altered the outlook of the average man. 'Never in the whole history of the world', it has been said, 'did so many people believe so firmly in so many things, the authority for which they could not test, as do Londoners to-day.' But, however this may be, in the history of the medieval church from the fifth century onwards the distinction between the sophisticated and the ignorant, though very marked, had not the particular significance which it has to-day. The most acute, disinterested, and sincere intellects were among the expositors of the Church. The issue did not lie between reason and faith. Rationalistic opposition to Christianity had by this time almost ceased to trouble the Church. Paganism abounded, but it was the literal paganism of the natural man, a force to be disciplined or an object of missionary enterprise, not an intellectual power capable of resistance and organized life. In the Middle Ages apologetic writing, with the exception of the *Summa contra Gentiles* of St. Thomas Aquinas, has not the importance in ecclesiastical literature possessed by the writings of the great Christian apologists or of St. Augustine: if we set on one side the numerous but subordinate tracts against Jews and Mohammedans, it was anything but defensive in character, it was rather an attempt to reach self-understanding. Civilized Europe was educated in a body of doctrine and enriched by a wealth of religious experience which were in conscious harmony with current conceptions of the universe. What resistance there was, so far as it was rooted in a life alien to Christianity, was ruthlessly suppressed. Like the plague, it was endemic, but, except for occasional epidemics of which the Albigensian heresy was the most severe, it was kept successfully out of sight, a monstrous unthinkable thing, abhorrent to the conscience of mankind. The few great heretics, such as Wyclif, did not base their objections to orthodox practice on principles unintelligible to the medieval mind; still less were they rationalists. They were extremists, urged by a strange medley of mood and circumstance to carry farther than others would a critical habit which was general in the great centres of learning. They went over the line which every man who thought for himself, and every man of ardent piety, was likely to approach, but from which all but they recoiled in horror.[1] Hence the problem of authority did

[1] Marsiglio of Padua in the fourteenth century was probably a 'rationalist' in the modern sense; but when the Pope compared Wyclif's doctrines with his, he was concerned with results, not with moods and processes. The sophistical disputations of the thirteenth and fourteenth centuries were deliberate acts of

not arise from a conflict between the faith of an organized Christendom and the reason of men outside the Church. It was not due, though this would be nearer the truth, to a conflict between reason within and faith without the Church. It was the problem of controlling the interplay within the Church of faith and reason, of religious experience and theology, the revelation and the interpretation of the purposes of God. Medieval theology was not stagnant; it sprang from intense religious feeling, and its function was to assist authority in the definition of dogma, as in the long discussions which preceded the definite assertion in 1216 of the doctrine of transubstantiation. It could even impose a long-disputed dogma upon the Church. The dogma of the Immaculate Conception of the Virgin, though left an open question by the Council of Trent and formally accepted by Pope Pius IX as late as 1854, was widely adopted after its reception by the English Benedictines, and, later, by the Franciscan theologian, Duns Scotus. On the other hand, theology might easily cross the line beyond which the general conscience, warned by tradition, refused to go. If there were few obstinate heretics in the Middle Ages, there were a great many persons who at one time or another were taxed with heresy. Nobody could feel safe unless he was prepared to rely in the last resort upon the judgement of the Church expressed through its authorized head. A pope, if he relied on his private judgement, could go astray and be called to book. The philosophical teaching of St. Thomas was watched with anxiety and was repudiated by many as charged with doctrine hostile to the faith. Heresy might assail the mystic as he sought to analyse the communion of the soul with God. And if, within the inner stronghold of the Church, apart from which life seemed incredible, dangers could beset the doctor and the saint, in how much greater danger was the multitude of ignorant men, undisciplined in the moral life, of the fanatics who could see but one ray of light at a time,

'playing with fire' and sometimes, notably in the case of the thoroughgoing Siger of Brabant, the disciple of Averroës, led to trouble; but, although important as a step towards the recognition of separate domains of faith and reason, they were not regarded very seriously, and the disputants rarely imagined that their conclusions could possess real validity.

of those immersed in social and economic life, distracted by ambition or pleasure or the precarious nature of their calling? Beyond the problem of authority lay the still greater problem of discipline, the task of finding some harmony between the Christian view of things and the life of the ordinary man.

How did it come about that the authority of the Church was so generally accepted as inseparable from the duties and aspirations of the Christian life? We now know enough about what used to be called the 'age of faith' to discount the conception of an obedient society, orderly to a point of unnatural self-suppression in everything relating to the government, the doctrine, the worship, the artistic interests of the Church. We no longer believe in that well-behaved body of the faithful, which, though essentially barbarous and ignorant, was always so sweetly submissive in its attitude to the mysteries of the Christian faith. Paganism in the Middle Ages was as endemic, speculation as bold, speech as pungent, the varieties of religious experience as numerous and as extravagant as at any time in the history of mankind. The state system of modern Europe, its nationalism, traditions of foreign policy, and strangely mixed ideas of right, force, utility can be traced back into the Middle Ages. Scholars who work among the repellent remains of late medieval scholasticism say that, hidden away in those unreadable manuscripts, are the germs of the mighty ideas of Leonardo da Vinci, Copernicus, Bruno, Spinoza. Luther fed his spirit on the writings of the Brethren of the Common Life; the intellectual ancestry of Hegel has been traced to the mystical philosophy of Eckhart. Can medieval Christianity, then, really have possessed the inner coherence which we have allowed to it? Ought we not to regard it as a complicated tyranny from which men were constantly striving to free themselves?

The answer to the view implied in these questions is, I think, twofold. In the first place the medieval Church was composed of societies rather than of individuals. Secondly, the sincerely religious person satisfied the needs of his inner life by adjusting himself to the interpretation of the world which the Church expounded.

1. Historically, the medieval Church, as distinct from the primitive Church, was composed of societies. If we look at the history of the spread of Christianity from the days of Constantine, we find that Christianity spread by the addition of masses of men, not by the conversion of particular people. There were some striking exceptions, but, generally speaking, the acceptance of Christianity was, to use a modern phrase, an affair of state, in which kings and other leaders, moved no doubt by missionaries and, as time went on, acting under the influence of the Pope, carried their subjects with them or imposed their will upon alien social groups. The success of the great St. Boniface in the eighth, and of the Cistercian monk, Christian of Oliva, in the thirteenth century was mainly due to the adherence of the local magnates and to the backing of friendly or interested powers outside. Boniface, for example, was more rapidly and permanently successful than had been the Celtic missionaries who preceded him in Germany, because he could rely upon Charles Martel in his organization of Thuringia and Hesse, and upon Duke Odilo in his organization of Bavaria. Christian of Oliva, the first bishop in Prussia (1212), had the support of the neighbouring duke of Masovia. The 'conversion' of Norway illustrates the drastic policy of a ruthless king. King Olaf Tryggvason proceeded methodically, province by province; and the *Heimskringla*, the later history of the kings of Norway, tells some profoundly interesting stories of the devotion to the old gods which he had to overcome, sometimes with almost incredible cruelty.[1] A religious system which originated in this way was, as in a more refined expression it has remained, a part of the social structure. Its organization was inextricably involved with that of the community. The powerful men who took pride in their work fostered and endowed it; they regarded resistance to it as an affront not only to God, but to society. The clergy had a recognized status in the tribal or national life; they sat in the courts, took cognizance of public affairs and private conduct,

[1] Laing, *Chronicle of the Kings of Norway* (1844), i. 427 ff. Evidence from other sources on the conversion of northern peoples is collected in Th. de Cauzons, *Histoire de l'Inquisition en France* (1909), i. 72 ff.

helped to shape the customs which they put into writing. Christianity, in general regard, though full of mystery, was not an alien or esoteric body of practice and belief; it rapidly became an inseparable element in men's lives, just as the old religions had been before it. We moderns are directly descended from these people, and our paganism, so far as it is unsophisticated, is the paganism of our forefathers, less crude and violent, but equally natural, equally consistent with a life of Christian conformity, which begins with baptism and closes with the solemn commitment of the body to the grave and the soul to the keeping of God. By paganism I mean a state of acquiescence, or merely professional activity, unaccompanied by sustained religious experience and inward discipline. It is not a state of vacancy and scepticism. It is confined to no class of persons, and is not hostile to, though it is easily wearied by, religious observance. It accepts what is offered without any sense of responsibility, has no sense of sin, and easily recovers from twinges of conscience. At the same time, it is full of curiosity and is easily moved by what is now called the group-mind. It is sensitive to the activities of the crowd, is often emotional, and can be raised to those moods of passion, superstition, and love of persecution into which religion, on its side, can degenerate. A medieval, like a modern, man remained a Christian because he was born a Christian, and most medieval Christians were probably men of this kind—not a few popes, cardinals, bishops, monks, friars, and parish clergy, and a large number of the clerks who had no cure of souls. The medieval Christian was, according to his lights, respectable. He was generally far too much interested in life, had too much to do, and was too affectionate, to be habitually cruel or sensual or superstitious. His life was inseparable from that of the community to which his Church gave a variety of colour, here radiant, there distressing. Although in periods of crisis he suffered decadence—sometimes widespread and horrible—casual decadence is more likely to have affected, not the conventional Christian, but the truly religious man.[1]

[1] For this aspect of medieval life see Coulton, *Five Centuries of Religion* (1923), vol. i, and Huizinga, *The Waning of the Middle Ages* (1924).

The history of the Church is the record of the gradual and mutual adaptation of Christianity and paganism to each other. The complete victory of the former has always been a remote vision. St. Paul's Epistles to the Corinthians show how the attempt to persuade their converts to put away earthly things taxed the patience and energy of the earliest apostles. The task became impossible when every member of any political community which possessed an ecclesiastical organization was supposed to be a follower of Christ. The influence of the Church penetrated social relations through and through, and it is foolish to feel surprise if Christianity suffered in the process. St. Boniface found that the German converts instinctively regarded baptism and the rites of the Church as forms of magic or merely external acts; [1] and his experience has countless parallels throughout the history of the Church up to our own day. The situation within the borders of the Roman Empire was especially perplexing. The lands around the Mediterranean were not merely full of superstition, they were intensely sophisticated, so that it is impossible to draw a sharp line between their superstition and their sophistry, between tradition and artifice, sincere piety and exotic faith.[2] The strange excesses which shocked St. Augustine and other ecclesiastical leaders in some of their fellow Christians were probably not very different from the psychical extravagance which had disgusted Cicero and Plutarch. Hence, as the Christian faith penetrated the society of the Roman world, it fell under the influence both of rustic traditions and of a variegated paganism which shaded off into those philosophical and mystical refinements so dear to the theologian. We are apt to forget that in the days of Christ the sea of Galilee was not like a silent Wastwater, lying solitary beneath the lonely hills, but was bordered by towns with temples and villas like the lakes of Geneva or Como to-day. From the first the Church was the victim as well as the victor, and as it absorbed the peoples of the Mediterranean in the west and spread eastwards into Persia and India, its spiritual life

[1] Hauck, *Kirchengeschichte Deutschlands*, i. 474 ff.

[2] See Dill, *Roman Society from Nero to Marcus Aurelius*, Book IV, c. 1, pp. 443 ff.

was shot through and through with the glittering fancies, the antinomianism, the morbid extravagances and the endless subtleties of men. It tried to purify a great sluice into which all the religions, every kind of philosophy, every remedy for the troubles and ennui of life had passed. And from this ordeal it passed on to cope with the mental and spiritual traditions of the great northern peoples. If we imagine that the Church was able to work upon a *tabula rasa*, we cannot understand the development either of its theology, its ritual, or its religious experience.

All this has long been familiar to students of the history of the early Church, and it is fairly familiar to those who study the interplay of Christianity and other traditions in the life of to-day; but it is still apt to puzzle us when we regard the Church in the Middle Ages. How did the medieval Church maintain a hold so hardly won in early times, so easily lost in our own? We must begin by realizing that, although its influence meant much more than this, the Church was the systematic expression of a life which had taken the place of the older religions. It was organized in dioceses of Roman or tribal origin; its ministers were not foreign enthusiasts, but men drawn from feudal and village society. The clergy, it is true, made claims upon the allegiance of their people which had no roots in natural ties and were independent of their personal worthiness. They were based on the truth that the kingdom of Christ is not of this world, and the really serious difficulties which the Church had to face were due to that ever-present spirit of anti-clericalism which was in part resistance to the claims of Christ, in part a sense of the contrast between Christ and his ministers. At the same time life on earth would never be comfortable, or even tolerable, if men had no way of grappling with its mysteries and terrors; and if they require protection against these, they must pay the price. On the whole the medieval pagans paid the price cheerfully. They paid tithes and dues. They allowed the clergy to receive their children into society at baptism, to define the limits within which marriage was permissible, to punish their sexual irregularities, to supervise the disposition of their goods by will, to guide their souls at the hour of death, and to bury their bodies. They recognized the obligations of confession, penance, communion. In one form or another much of the discipline was as old as society; there must be initiation, regulation, and ceremonial in human relations if men and women are to live together; and, on the other hand, it was not altogether as though the widespreading, penetrating, exotic life of the Church was not largely in their own keeping. It was their own brothers and cousins who crowned and anointed kings, ruled bishoprics and monasteries, and celebrated in their churches—the churches which they themselves had built or helped to maintain. Strangers might bring in new fashions and new knowledge, but their successors would be men drawn from themselves. It was all very interesting: the Church gave them very much, and yet they were at the same time inside the Church. They were both spectators and actors. They got wonderful buildings, pictures, plays, festivals, stories full of apocryphal detail about Biblical heroes and saints; but they could themselves help to build, paint, perform, repeat. They gibed incessantly at the clergy with their hypocrisy, venality, immorality, yet they had a good deal of sympathy with them, for they were of their own flesh. The real enemies were the cranks and heretics who would not play the game.

What we call abuses or superstition in the medieval Church were part of the price paid for, not obstacles to, its universality. They were due to the attempt of pagans to appropriate a mystery. If the people paid, so did the Church. We distort the facts if we try to separate clergy and laity too sharply, for paganism was common to both. Medieval thinkers and reformers saw this far more clearly than we can, and were never tired of discussing the problem. In the eleventh century Cardinal Peter Damiani pointed out in his lurid way that it was of no use to try to keep the clergy apart from the laity unless strict evangelical poverty were insisted upon for all clergy alike. But Damiani and all the preachers of Apostolic poverty who came after him were caught on the horns of a dilemma. If it is the function of the Church to drive out sin, it must separate itself from sin; if the Church separates itself from sin, it becomes a clique. The Church took another course. Under the guidance of austere pontiffs like Gregory VII and Innocent III it embarked upon an intensive policy of discipline, whose basis was the very claim to universality. To Innocent III the dilemma was clear enough—few men have been so tortured by reflections upon the misery of mankind—but he was a statesman and lawyer, prepared to deal with realities as he found them. By his time (he was a contemporary of our King John) it was too late to go back. As an ecclesiastical system the body of Christ was becoming the most intricate administration which the world had yet seen; as a society the Church affected and was affected by every form of human endeavour. From the one point of view the distinction between lay and clerical is all-important; from the other it is irrelevant. The secular influences which played upon sacred things did not work through the laity alone. Certainly the men of outstanding piety and wisdom were generally to be found among the clergy, the militia of Christ; but the wind bloweth where it listeth: the pope might be a pagan at heart, the beggar a saint.

In the fifth century Basil, the local bishop, described in his book on the miracles of St. Thecla the conversation of the pilgrims who gathered for the feast of the saint at Seleucia. The visitors, sitting around a table, exchange their impressions.

> 'One is astonished by the magnificence and splendour of the ceremonies, another by the vast crowds which they have attracted, a third by the large concourse of bishops. One praises the eloquence of the preachers, another the beauty of the psalmody, another the endurance of the public during the long night office, another the fine arrangement of the services, another the fervour in prayer of the assistants. One recalls the dust, another the stifling heat, while yet another has observed the coming and going during the holy mysteries, how so-and-so went out, and how another returned and went away again, the cries and disputes, the disorder of people getting into each other's way and refusing to give place, each eager to be the first to participate.'[1]

In a few words this picture describes the attitude of the

[1] See Delehaye, 'Les recueils antiques de miracles des saints', in *Analecta Bollandiana* (1925), xliii. 56–7.

faithful during the history of the Church. Add to the feast of a saint or martyr, the pilgrimages and jubilees, the ceremonies of corporate life, the coronation of kings, the initiation into knighthood, the passion and miracle plays, the propaganda and conduct of a crusade, the passage at any time through the countryside of a popular preacher, and we have the circumstances in which the 'group mind' was affected in the Middle Ages. Add, again, the churches and cathedrals with their descriptive or symbolic ritual, sculpture, wall-painting, and we have the material forms which, so to speak, 'fixed' the belief and imagination of the medieval Christian. An excitement of the senses accompanied the appeal of the spirit. One need not look farther than the clerical class. From the little boys in the bishop's household to the bishop himself they felt with an infinite variety of intensity that they were members of a great professional body, but the conditions of their life would make them partisans—attached to their particular 'use', eager for the success of their patron saint, anxious about their revenues, ready to fight on behalf of the views of their favourite teachers. The mixture of motives which in a few was a source of shame was in the many a sanction of self-confidence and corporate feeling. In the particular form in which this natural expression of human nature affects our modern world, it is a legacy from the conditions under which the Church developed in the Middle Ages, under the spacious opportunities opened up by a universal society.

The interaction of theological subtlety and popular credulity had cruder and more dangerous effects. Perhaps the most striking example is its effect upon the system of indulgences. In its purest form the theory underlying the indulgence was a fine one. It was inspired by the writings of St. Paul and was safeguarded by the maxim of the Fathers, *Quod homo non punit, Deus punit*. The system itself was a natural development of the penitential system and was related to the power of absolution. Its justification was found, in the climax of a long discussion among canonists and theologians, in the doctrine of the treasure stored up by saints and martyrs and all good Christians, who, a great body of friends, combine to help the erring. But it was extremely difficult to avoid misconception and abuse. Some of the theological terms, notably the term 'remission of sins', were misleading; some of the preachers of indulgences were ignorant or headstrong or unscrupulous. Warfare had constantly to be waged by bishops and universities against the belief that not punishment, but sin itself, was remitted, or that indulgences could benefit the dead as well as the living. The system encouraged fantastic and heterodox views about the unlimited powers of the Pope, or profitless discussions on the nature of purgatory; and in some directions popular pressure proved too strong for the theologians, so that later speculation far outran the cautious handling of the subject by the great scholastics.[1]

2. We have seen that the pagan paid homage to the faith. The Church coloured his whole life and did so very rightly, because, so men vaguely felt, it interpreted life. Its secret was not merely part of life, it gave meaning to life, and was the spring of that knowledge of the universe of which the Church was the vehicle. Profane knowledge, as it is so strangely called, was certainly of value only in so far as it led men to understand higher truth, yet it was not alien, not the property of teachers outside the Church. Hence we can never be sure that the absurdities and abuses of Christendom were unmixed with fine emotion. Over against the brutal criticism at the expense of ecclesiastics and their agents we must set the fact that every activity fell in some degree under clerical influence, and in doing so could be touched to finer issues. The history of chivalry gives us many examples. Pilgrims on the way to Rome or Compostella stayed in churches and monasteries whose inmates repeated tales and legendary incidents which were worked up into the *chansons de geste*. At the end of the twelfth century the Arthurian legend was refined by the noble improvisation of the Holy Grail, so that a suggestion, drawn originally perhaps from the apocryphal gospel of Nicodemus, gave the story of Parsival to the literature of chivalry. The theme of 'courteous love'[2] was developed

[1] Paulus, *Geschichte des Ablasses im Mittelalter*, e.g. i. 288 ff.; ii. 170 ff., 197 ff.; iii. 376 ff.

[2] On its origins, which were neither Christian nor northern, see Christopher Dawson, *Mediaeval Religion* (1934), pp. 107–13, 126 ff.

under the influence of mystical experience and even of the logical methods of the schools, for the poets who turned from the exaltation of brutal passion to praise unselfish devotion to woman had been affected, we are told, by the cult of the Virgin and by theological elaborations of the meaning of 'Charitas'. Many delicate filaments bound the new chivalry to the unseen world. And this being so, it would be unwise to deny the existence of an unselfish note in the response to all the inducements which were offered to men and women to abstain from sin; and we should be rash to assume that those who adopted as a career the task of offering the inducements to their neighbours were unvisited by the sense of their high calling. However professional their attitude, even if they looked upon holy mysteries as things which could be bought and sold, this was only possible because they believed that their calling and their wares were part of a divine economy, interpreting the very nature of things. Had this belief not been general, there might have been a revolt, but never a Reformation.

There is no clear border-line in the region of religious experience between the swamps and jungle of paganism and the sunlit uplands of pure faith. St. Francis was not without a speck, and there was doubtless a glimmering of piety in the relic-mongers who traded in pigs' bones. But we have no difficulty in distinguishing the pagan from the saint when we see them. We can recognize throughout the history of the Church, in all ranges of society, the presence of men and women to whom Christianity, as interpreted by the Church, gave the highest satisfaction possible to human nature. In the Middle Ages the hold of the Church was due to the fact that it could satisfy the best cravings of the whole man, his love of beauty, his desire for goodness, his endeavour after truth. In these days the demand for certainty is distracted by conflicting claims. In the Middle Ages it was not so: the divine mystery was felt to inspire a divine order in which all knowledge and all emotion could be reconciled. Of course, if we insist with cold objectivity on drawing out the implications of the religious experience or of the philosophical systems of sincere men, they will rarely fit the mould. Regarded in this way St.

Augustine, Dante, Eckhart, are probably as intractable as Spinoza or Milton or Goethe. St. Thomas himself helped to open a door which the Church has tried in vain to close. We can no more estimate the measure of acquiescence between the Church and its members in the lives of saints and theologians than we can in the secret moods of its humbler children. The Church is constantly hastening after the saints, so that in learning from them it may also control them. But these spiritual discrepancies are signs of healthy life so long as the vigorous souls, however restless and independent they may be, continue to find their satisfaction in the Church. In the Middle Ages nearly all men of this type gave themselves whole-heartedly. The teaching of the Church did no lasting violence to their experience, doubts, misgivings, for in communion with the Church they found their highest satisfaction. Dante says:

'Human longing is measured in this life by that degree of knowledge which it is here possible to possess; and that point is never transgressed except by misapprehension which is beside the intention of nature. . . . And this is why the saints envy not one another, because each one attains the goal of his longing, which longing is commensurate with the nature of his excellence.'[1]

This satisfaction was possible because men felt that they and all their social and spiritual affinities were part of the divine order inspired by the unfathomable mystery. They appropriated a body of truth in which, if they adjusted themselves to it, they felt sure of harmony, and to rebellion from which they traced the sin and misery of mankind. I cannot discuss here the principles of this order, to be found in the physical structure of earth and heavens, in the harmony of all law, natural and social, in the dovetailing of the disconnected learning, true or false, about men, beasts, birds, plants, minerals, into a scheme combined of Biblical and classical suggestion. It is enough to point out that although most of the medieval cosmology and chronology have gone, the medieval view of the universe lasted a very long time and has by no means altogether disappeared. The medieval philosophy of history has not ceased to influence us. It was deduced from three sources, the Biblical

[1] *Il Convito*, iii, c. 15, trans. Wicksteed.

chronology harmonized with that of non-Jewish peoples by Eusebius, the Augustinian theory of the city of God and its later developments, the idea of the *preparatio evangelica*, which took its finest form in Dante's conception of the provision of the Roman Empire by the Father, with its universal peace as a cradle for His Son. The Eusebian chronology, revised by Archbishop Ussher in the seventeenth century, has indeed gone, but in its simplest expression the conception of the preparation for the gospel is a living part of Christian thought. The belief that the earth is the centre of the stellar system has gone, but the anthropocentric ideas bound up with it are dying very hard. The zoology of the medieval mind was fantastic, but it was due not to lack of intelligence, but to lack of observation, and could not be regarded as absurd so long as distinct species were held to be the results of separate acts of creation. Underlying the strange parallels between the truths of revelation and the phenomena of the natural world was that sense of rhythm in the universe, whose philosophical expression has a very respectable origin in Greek thought and a destiny which would seem to be increasing in grandeur. In a word, medieval thought was at bottom anything but absurd. It was pursued with an ability which would find no difficulty in coping with the problems of modern science and speculation. And it reached forward to a mystical reception of God, in whom is the ordered union of all the objects of knowledge, natural and revealed, human and divine. The great mystics, indeed, boldly urged that for this very reason the search after God under settled forms is futile. Eckhart once said:

> 'He who fondly imagines to get more of God in thoughts, prayers, pious offices and so forth, than by the fireside or in the stall: in sooth he does but take God, as it were, and swaddle his head in a cloak and hide him under the table. For he who seeks God under settled forms lays hold of the form while missing the God concealed in it.'

And the same Master Eckhart, the Dominican contemporary of Dante, also said:

> 'Man has to seek God in error and forgetfulness and foolishness.

For deity has in it the power of all things and no thing has the like. The sovran light of the impartible essence illumines all things. St. Dionysius says that beauty is good order with pre-eminent lucidity. Thus God is an arrangement of three Persons. And the soul's lower power should be ordered to her higher, and her higher ones to God; her outward senses to her inward and her inward ones to reason: thought to intuition and intuition to the will and all to unity, so that the soul may be alone with nothing flowing into her but sheer divinity, flowing here into itself.'[1]

Eckhart lived at a time when the best strength of the Church was expended in the codification of law and discipline and doctrine, and, although he was suspect, as probing too deep, and some of his teaching was condemned after his death, he reminds us that the Church was more than a pedagogue, that it was a school in which the ignorant and the learned worked together at a common task. Stripped of all accessories the task of the Church was the elucidation, in thought and life, of the divine mystery as revealed in the Bible, all other texts and tools being subsidiary. The Bible has rightly been called the text-book of the Middle Ages. It was studied, of course, in Latin, the version partly compiled but very largely made by St. Jerome being the standard text or Vulgate. The canons of its interpretation, unfortunately not so good as those laid down by Jerome, were defined by St. Augustine. The standard commentary, drawn from the Fathers, and afterwards known as the Gloss, was the outcome of a gradual process of elucidation, which culminated in the twelfth century. The Gloss underlies all later work and influenced every medieval exposition, including that in stone and on glass. The text of the Vulgate was revised by Alcuin, in the days of Charles the Great, and one descendant of this revision was later adopted by the teachers of Paris as an official text, about the time when it was divided into chapters by Stephen Langton (*c.* 1200). Dominicans and others provided it with critical apparatus and concordances. The authority of the Bible was final—it was an isolated and unsuccessful vagary of St. Bernard that he regarded the

[1] *Meister Eckhart*, Pfeiffer's edition, trans. Evans (London, 1924), pp. 39–40, 49.

text as subject to the decision of the Church—and no more damaging charge could be levelled against a group of theologians than that it gave too little attention to scriptural study. No more perplexing problem could present itself than an apparent inconsistency between the teaching of the Bible and the general consensus of the Church. When Pope John XXII, preaching, as he was careful to say, not as Pope but as a simple priest, taught his heretical doctrine of the Beatific Vision, he based his case upon the supreme authority of Scripture.[1] He bowed before the opposition of the theologians, and it was reserved for Wyclif to give reality to the great question whether the Church is or is not to be regarded as the final authority in interpretation.

Here we come to an issue even more intractable than that between property and evangelical poverty. The greatest danger to the Church lay neither in dogma, nor in the hierarchy, nor in the interpretation of the world ; it lay in the inner experience of men who received all these things as a matter of course, and in whom the Church had for centuries found its strength. They had felt the impact of Christ, and, as time wore on, they found their way to Christ more and more through the Scriptures. As it strained to understand the truth in its mysterious inheritance and to relate it to the rest of experience, the Church had encouraged a strange variety of thought and self-conscious religious life. Both the thought and the spiritual experience of the Middle Ages were destined to have a great future, within and without the Church. As we draw nearer to modern times, we feel that they were gaining an independent strength, a sense of confidence, a sanction within themselves stronger than the sanctions by which they had previously been directed. Just as the problem of the power of the Church had been narrowed down to the issue of poverty, so the problem of authority was at bottom the issue whether goodness and sincerity were their own sanctions. The issue is logically insoluble and has shattered Christendom. In the interests of order and unity the Church had been able to control the zealots who urged that the guardians

[1] See Noel Valois's life of John XXII in *Histoire littéraire de la France*, xxxiv, notably pp. 559–67, 606.

and teachers of the faith should have no worldly ties: it had found room for all kinds of communities, from the well-ordered and tolerant Benedictines to the severest types of asceticism; it had even rallied them all to its defence, so that its richly brocaded garments were, as it were, upheld by mendicants. If they were restless or developed antinomian tendencies, the teachers of poverty were suppressed. There is no more poignant symbol of the unequal conflict than the handful of spiritual Franciscans urging their cause at the magnificent court of the popes at Avignon. But the issue raised by sane and well-balanced religious experience—the issue of conscience, so closely related to that of poverty—was a more difficult matter to deal with. The more orthodox it was, the more dangerous it was. Wyclif was a truly portentous figure, but he was too solitary, too subtle and dogmatic, to be a lasting menace. The Hussites of Bohemia were prophetic of the national churches which were to come, but, hidden away in a corner, and distracted by social and political aspirations, they could be controlled or placated. The real danger lay in the quiet, active, mystical men and women who, in the face of evil around them, began to think and to experience for themselves the implications of fellowship with Christ. They were not concerned with vexed questions of interpretation, but with the immediate appeal of the Bible and of the life of prayer. To them so much which, in the eyes of ecclesiastics and lawyers, was all-important, seemed trivial, the basis of their faith so much more essential than the superstructure, the sense of fellowship in the sacraments and prayer more urgent than the explanation of the mysterious.[1] There is nothing heterodox in this, unless it be the tendency to insist that the validity of a spiritual act depends upon the fitness of him who performs it. Recent apologists have shown how the experiences of the later mystics can be linked with the teaching of the twelfth-century mystics, St. Bernard and the school of St. Victor. Yet, notably through the schools of the Brethren of the Common Life in the Rhineland, the movement was strong enough to influence the life not only

[1] Cf. the chapter in the *Imitatio Christi* on nice disputes regarding the Lord's Supper, Book IV, c. 18.

of Ignatius Loyola, the founder of the Jesuits, but of Calvin, and indirectly of Luther.[1]

How the growth of ordered, self-controlled piety, affecting clergy and laity in little nests of spiritual contentment, could have results so striking in their diversity is one of the most fascinating problems in history. The movement seemed so hopeful, yet was so devastating in its effects. It is no part of my task to try to explain this problem, except to point out that its solution is clearly connected with the contemporary growth of an equally ordered and self-controlled secularism. This spirit of secularism affected the organized Church hardly less than the 'national states'. Piety and paganism, so to speak, came to their own and tried to settle their differences in new ways. The dream of a united Christendom, in which paganism would be transformed under the beneficent guidance of the official disciples of Christ, was seen to have been a dream. The Church had tried to control and never ceased to influence the world, but it could not identify the world with the Church in one Kingdom of God. The world had its own claims—claims of nationality, of the interplay of capital and labour, of trade, of social expression. Perhaps the issue is best summed up in the words of a Florentine chronicler who lived in the days of Boniface VIII and Philip the Fair, of Master Eckhart and Dante: 'Humility is of no avail against sheer evil.'[2]

Many historians have traced the gradual emergence into separate life in the fourteenth and fifteenth centuries of the forces, hitherto inextricably connected, of political self-direction and an elaborate ecclesiastical organism no longer able, in their struggle for existence, to control the life of the spirit. But they have written in the light of four centuries of later history. For the ordinary man, were he devout or pagan at heart, life in those times must still have

[1] See especially Albert Hyma, *The Christian Renaissance* (Michigan and The Hague, 1924). Like the Friends of God before them, Groote and his followers protested against anything over-subtle or antinomian.

[2] The words are 'Niente vale l'humiltà contra alla grande malizia'. Dino Compagni is meditating on the futility of self-effacing moderation in the civil strife of the Italian cities. Cf. below, pp. 100–1, for the philosophical side of the issue.

been full of colour and adventure in a world which nothing could shake. If we go to-day into Winchester cathedral, we can still recapture the sense of that ordered, that magnificent stability. Sheltered by the massive Norman walls and the intricate Gothic roof, the effigies of the ecclesiastics lie—Edington, Wykeham, Beaufort, Waynflete, Fox, prelates and statesmen, each in his painted, delicately chiselled shrine. Those tombs are a symbol of security. Those men lived in times full of perplexity, but undisturbed by any feelings of catastrophe. In their world heresy and antinomianism could have no abiding place. We realize why the call of Master Eckhart, deep thinker though he was, to withdraw oneself to commune with God in the ground of the soul, died away in secret, why the visionary prophecies of the Joachimites passed like whispers in the undergrowth, why the Friends of God and the Brethren of the Common Life were half contemptuously welcomed as harmless pietists who performed a useful function, why Wyclif's academic influence withered so quickly. The sense of reality was still to be found in the conventional ways so full of colour and movement. There were few times and places during the last centuries of the Middle Ages in which the adventurous soul could not find intimations of the great opportunities for mind and spirit made possible by organized Christianity. The awakening might come slowly, or be arrested in some career in which the sense of vocation was dormant. But we must not believe that all lingered in the outer courts.

> Expertus potest credere
> Quid sit Iesum diligere.

II

Hitherto we have been trying to understand the atmosphere of medieval Christianity, how it worked in an undeveloped society, fundamentally pagan. Christianity was presented through the Church as an interpretation of the universe, but still more as the living operation of divine providence. It was established as an essential element in the social order, and yet it called men to the greatest of adventures, the service and contemplation of God. It could give excitement to the frivolous, occupation of every kind, physical or intellectual or contemplative, to the serious; and it could offer opportunities in high places as in low to the depraved. It engaged the highest faculties in co-operation with the purpose of God by satisfying their craving for an ordered and just interpretation of life. In the Church human self-esteem was gratified: *nam non ecclesia propter coelum, sed propter ecclesiam coelum*. Through the Church man could escape from his sense of frustration by dedicating himself to the glory of God.

Something should now be said about the organization in which, as a self-protective and directing force, the ideals of Christian society expressed themselves. For here, and notably in the earlier history of the papacy, we may find the highest attempt to give concrete and permanent shape to the energy, the audacity, love of order and austerity which played with such bewildering freedom in the medieval world.

The centralization of the Western Church under one head satisfied in large measure the desire for unity, order, peace, righteousness. The most fruitful influence in expressing this desire was undoubtedly the great bishop of Hippo, St. Augustine, to whose thought the famous Pope Gregory the Great did most to give currency.[1] St. Augustine was not concerned with the papal power. It is not easy, indeed, to say how far he was concerned to maintain that the organized Church was the only expression on earth of the City of God. Just as he hesitated in his analysis of the grounds of secular authority, so he hesitated to admit that the truth might not lie with faithful souls who had been forced to suffer in silence through the errors or misunderstanding of ecclesiastical authority. His writings were very various, and when, like the *De Civitate Dei*, they were written over a period of many years, they are not perfectly coherent. The important matter is that Augustine's philosophy of history became the main source of papal apologetic. Its central thought is the harmony which exists in

[1] For what follows I am indebted particularly to the writings of Bernheim and an article by Hauck, 'Die Rezeption und Umbildung der allgemeinen Synode im Mittelalter' (*Historische Vierteljahrschrift*, 1907).

the society at peace with itself in the enjoyment of God. This harmony—so others drew out his meaning—affects the whole of nature. It is not a quality which is added, rather it is acquiescence in something eternally true and real. It is not like the 'pax Romana'. In one passage of his book (xxii. 6) St. Augustine discusses the view, set out by Cicero in his *De Republica*, that no good state will engage in war unless for the sake of safety or in order to keep faith; and he shows that in the earthly state this view involves a possible contradiction, for Cicero regards permanence as the mark of the state, and in order to keep itself alive a state may have to sacrifice its good faith for the sake of safety. But the safety of the City of God is maintained or, rather, acquired with and through faith; if faith is lost, salvation is impossible. This argument is not merely a play upon the word, *salus*, *fides*, for in the City of God the faith and salvation of the individual are bound up with the order of a society which has its permanence and its understanding in God. The next stage in the argument is that the supreme active quality of a state of harmony is *iustitia* or righteousness, while the prime cause of resistance to it is pride, the vice which for this reason, that it breaks up the peace of communion in the enjoyment of God, came to be regarded in later days as the worst of the seven deadly sins. So, finally, we can understand the deep significance of the insistence upon justice in the political thought of the Middle Ages. The just ruler, whether he be pope or king, is not merely one who deals fairly; he is the one whose righteousness proves his kingdom to be part of the harmony of things. The unjust ruler is a tyrant, the victim of pride which sets itself against this harmony. When a tyrant holds sway, a touch of confusion disturbs the whole of nature. A shiver runs through the world, as when the veil of the Temple was rent in twain at the time of the Crucifixion. The medieval chroniclers who drew dire conclusions from times of plague, famine, loss of crops and herds, violent storms and sudden death, paid homage, by no means always unconscious homage, to this conviction. Conversely, if justice prevails, all is at peace. This belief became a theme for high speculation, as in Dante's vision of the

Empire, and survived to inspire Milton's 'Ode on the Morning of Christ's Nativity'.

What may seem to us poetic fancy was an incentive to action. It gave a direction to policy as clearly as the teaching of the Stoics did in earlier times or as the doctrine of Karl Marx has done in our own day. And it influenced some of the most powerful men who ever lived. We do wrong to popes like Gregory the Great, and Gregory VII, and Innocent III, if we regard them only as statesmen or lawyers; and it is quite beside the point to accuse them of inconsistency, to collect, for example, Gregory VII's letters about peace and justice, and to set over against them the devastating effects of his conflict with the Emperor Henry IV. By Gregory VII's time the visible Church on earth, under the guidance of the Pope, had become the accepted embodiment of the City of God, carrying with it all the high responsibilities which the maintenance of the divine order involved. The Church set its face against any distinction, in the sense of any possible lack of continuity, between the Church visible and invisible.[1] Righteousness must be tempered with mercy and gentleness; it was inconceivable without them; but it must insist on obedience to the rule of order and beat down the proud. The just ruler must be humble, remembering that the inequalities of man are due to sin and that all men are by nature equal, yet he has a trust from God and must not shirk the responsibility of conflict, even if it means the use of force and the sword, against evil.

In the next place, the papacy satisfied the desire for guidance and certainty. The absence of contact in the second and third centuries between the adventurous theologian and the mass of believers has frequently been noted. There was no strong middle element, and the learned, whose profound religious experience was refined and made aware of itself by philosophical contemplation, tended to regard themselves as the guardians of the heavenly treasure, the message entrusted to the Church. The things hidden from the wise, by which God made foolish the wisdom of the world (1 Cor. i. 20), were now, in the opinion of many, the things hidden

[1] Cf. the decrees of the Council of Trent, session xxiii, c. 1.

by the wise. That this tendency, which many leaders deplored, was checked in the West, and the speculations of the theologians put to the test of the experience of the simple, was largely due to the leadership of the bishops of Rome.[1] In their categorical expressions of witness to the faith, free from dialectic and erudition, the popes began their spacious task of registering the growth of religious and ecclesiastical experience. It would be impossible to say how far they declared a general will, and out of place to try to estimate their authority in the days of the great councils. But the foundations of papal power were laid in these acts of authoritative testimony to the faith of the common man. One of the great poets of the Church, St. Paulinus of Nola (d. 431), the rich senator and landowner who gave up his wealth for Christ, spoke the mind of the West when he said, 'In omnem fidelem Spiritus Dei spirat'.

To describe the growth of papal leadership would be to write the history of the Church during the next eleven hundred years. The ecclesiastical organization of Rome itself was followed by the gradual penetration, in the West, of the *ordo romanus*, that is to say, of Roman liturgical uses, &c. The inclusion in Christendom of new peoples and areas under the joint influence of papal and secular authority involved the development of a disciplinary system: violence and passion had to be curbed, and barbarian habits subdued to the moral law of Christ. The penitentials with their codes of offences and punishments were one of the bases of the great system of canon law which was elaborated in a long series of handbooks and culminated in the *Decretum* of Gratian and the later codifications of decretals. The growth of the canon law was made possible by the work of provincial councils, by papal decrees and schools of jurisprudence, most of all, perhaps, by the development of diocesan administration. The history of these movements is very uneven. Local authority, whether clerical or lay, did not acquiesce easily and uniformly in the tendency to refer difficult matters to Rome, while the moral authority

[1] See, for example, the remarks of J. Lebreton on the action of Dionysius of Rome, in a remarkable article, 'La foi populaire et la théologie savante', *Revue d'histoire ecclésiastique* (1924), xx, p. 9 note; and, generally, pp. 33–7.

of the papacy was frequently disturbed by faction in Rome itself and by the depravity of the successors of St. Peter. But in course of time the issue became clear. Reformers, whose moral sense was shocked by the subjection of spiritual life to the accidents of local caprice or secular interests, at last threw their influence on the side of centralized authority. The local hierarchy, so jealous of its rights, found that its freedom was better secured by submission to the higher authority of Rome than by uneasy co-operation with princes. The organization at head-quarters of a college of cardinals as an electoral and advisory body, the increasing employment of papal legates who, like the *missi dominici* of Charles the Great and the itinerant justices of our English kings, distributed the authority of their master, gave coherence and uniformity to the exercise of papal power; the swollen stream of appeals and references to Rome hastened the steady elaboration of a common administrative system. The climax came at the beginning of the thirteenth century, when Innocent III gave definite expression to the theory of the *plenitudo potestatis* of the Pope, and, consciously reverting to the age of the great councils of Nicaea and Chalcedon, summoned an oecumenical council in which he restated the faith, in some degree codified the practice of the Church, and expounded a policy for the future.

Historians in a one-sided way often deal with this development as though it were nothing but a striving after papal infallibility, or a victory of personal ambition working with the aid of forged documents. The traditions of protestant controversy were reinforced by Döllinger's anonymous tract, 'The Pope and the Council' (1869), a powerful criticism of the ultramontane ideas which were so hotly debated before and during the Vatican Council of 1870. However effectively this famous tract may appeal to us as a discussion of an ecclesiastical problem, it is not altogether happy as an interpretation of the Middle Ages. It suggests a perpetual cleavage between the central court of Christendom and Christendom itself.[1] Other historians have been unduly impressed by the drastic criticism to which

[1] I do not deny, of course, that the doctrine of the papal power became increasingly definite. Its history was made clear by Schulte in 1871.

medieval writers subjected the Curia; they forget that men do not attack so persistently the abuses of an unnecessary tribunal, and they do not always point out that the criticism was not accompanied by any hint of schism. The denunciation of the delays, extortions, and venality of the papal court was an indirect tribute to its actuality. The work done by the Curia was enormous, ranging from arbitrations between kings to minute regulations about disputes in a parish. The Pope, needless to say, could not transact all this business unaided. His chancery became the most technical and also the most efficient administrative machine which had ever existed. Every stage in the preparation of a bull or mandate was carefully scrutinized to secure authenticity, prevent forgery, and guarantee that each formality, from the acquiescence of the pontiff to the consideration of technical objections by the parties, had been observed. And the preparation of a papal bull was merely the culmination of judicial process or of deliberation in council. When papal attention was most deeply engaged, the Pope naturally had recourse to his advisers, and asked the opinion of theologians and canonists. As the unworthy exponent of divine justice, he was expected to purge his mind of caprice and prejudice. The medieval mind, indeed, was much perplexed by the possibility of error in the interpretation of the will of God. It spent much labour in the invention of expedients and rules for distinguishing between the true and the false. The subtle dialectic, the procedure of the inquisition, the process of canonization had at least one object in common, the circumvention of the powers of evil. The Devil and his agents were everywhere, waiting to take advantage of mankind, which since the Fall had been so exposed to the wiles of duplicity. The great mercy of God is necessary, said St. Augustine, to secure that he who thinks he has good angels for friends, has not evil spirits as false friends. If we consider the vast literature of miracles and visions which meet us in the lives of the saints we may well believe that tests were necessary, and cease to marvel that they were often so ineffective. And if we are amazed at the credulity which could accept the revelations of a casual epileptic and at the incredulity which could denounce as suggestions of demons the visions of Joan of Arc, we should remember that, in accordance with belief in the fundamental necessity of unity and order, tests would especially be applied to those crucial cases, which seemed to involve the safety of the community, to detect pride and disobedience. For every power was subject to law. The Pope himself was not secure, for he was bound by the decisions of the Fathers and the great councils. He might err; he might be condemned for heresy. His moral lapses, his administrative errors, it is true, were matters for God alone, but the most unflinching papalists were agreed that his dogmatic errors were a matter for the Church. In one of his sermons Innocent III dealt with the possibility that he might err in the faith, and declared that in such a case he could be judged by the Church; and his view was sustained by later canonists and theologians.

Lastly, the growth of the papal power permitted within a united Church the development of a richer life. The history of the Church between the fifth and the thirteenth centuries reveals two tendencies, opposed in their natural operation, yet reconciled to a remarkable degree under the guidance of the hierarchy. The appropriation of Christianity by the vigorous, half-civilized peoples of western Europe resulted in spiritual and intellectual ferment, in a luxuriant growth of spiritual experience which manifested itself in religious associations, in speculation, in various forms of piety and superstition. But, in contrast with these phenomena, the spread of Christianity was directed by men, leaders in an organized community, who were inspired by the ideas of Cyprian, Ambrose, and Augustine. Conversion, in this view, was not an opportunity for free thought, but a call to duty in an ordered world. The varieties of experience were not repressed, but they were disciplined, so that the life of the Church was enriched, and not distracted, by monastic experiments, by the reception of neo-platonic theology, by the impetus of Greek and Arabic learning. Scope was allowed for the awakened energies of mind and spirit which, if undirected, have in all ages retarded progress in one direction as much as they have advanced it in another.[1]

[1] A useful introduction to the chief types of medieval heresy will be found in

The medieval methods of cultivation and restraint are not in favour nowadays, but if we reflect upon the magnitude of the task, the condition of society and the amazing energy of its life in the early Middle Ages, it cannot justly be said that they were unduly repressive. And, by maintaining as a practical guide in life the conception of an ordered universe, in which there is a fundamental harmony between moral and physical law, the Church turned the faces of the European peoples in the only direction along which social and scientific advance was possible.

New movements within the Church reacted upon the idea of the Church. During the early period there was an inevitable tendency in ordinary speech, if not in theological thought, to narrow the conception of the Church. 'Little man, why is your head shaved?' says a heathen champion to the Pope in one of the *chansons de geste*. The contrast between the Church, represented by a handful of clergy, and the still reluctant world was still so striking. The same tendency may be seen in the great struggles between the lay and clerical powers. As late as the end of the twelfth century great popes like Alexander III and Innocent III speak at times as though episcopate and church were synonymous terms. But by this time the scriptural view, summed up by the Fathers and always maintained by theologians, had acquired renewed significance in the development of all kinds of ecclesiastical activity. It is often said that the conception of the Church was narrowed by the growth of a papal tyranny. This is not a correct analysis of the subsequent unrest. The idea of the Church as the whole body of the faithful could only acquire such measure of reality as it ever has acquired through the growth of organized life which accompanied the growth of papal influence. The Church as a body of clergy and laity conscious of their membership in Christ, and at the same time coincident with the whole of European society in the West, did in fact come nearer to realization in the days of the Crusades, of the revived Benedictine movements, of Abelard and St. Bernard, Gratian and Petrus Lombardus than in

Alphandéry's *Les Idées morales chez les hétérodoxes latins au début du XIIIe siècle* (1903).

any other period in its history. The conception was developed with magnificent elaboration in the writings of Hugh of St. Victor.

How, borne down by the heavy weight of intricate, incessantly more intricate, machinery, torn asunder by the conflicting motion of its adventurous life, the Church failed to maintain agreement with this view of things, it would require an essay much longer than the present to explain. In the eyes of many the Church has seemed but to relax its hold in order to secure itself more firmly. To others its history in the Middle Ages is the record of the greatest of all human efforts to find that certainty, that something out of life, which 'while it is expected is already gone—has passed unseen, in a sigh, in a flash—together with the youth, with the strength, with the romance of illusions'.

II

DANTE AND THE CRUSADE[1]

DURING Dante's lifetime the Crusade was a live issue in men's minds. Although some regarded it as folly and many regarded it with indifference, few, if any, would have admitted that the days of the Crusade were over. It might be described in modern terms with much justice as the basis of public policy, as the immediate objective which made unity of urgent importance in the Church militant on earth, as inextricably bound up with the ways in which the unity of the West had been secured under papal direction. It had come in the course of time to give meaning to public life and to justify public policy, so that the idea of it was accepted as a matter of course. In modern times, religious and social ideals have, in a similar way, become within a few generations not merely ideals but mental and moral habits of certain groups of men and women, so that the very thought of disloyalty to them is shocking. George Meredith described a young idealist of this type in his *Beauchamp's Career*. If we were to imagine for a moment that the League of Nations had managed to exist for two hundred years, that it had made several impressive, though only partly successful, demonstrations against what were regarded as forces of evil, had contrived fiscal and administrative machinery with a view to these activities, and had developed forms of speech and thought which had become ingrained in the minds even of the least submissive, we should have a rough analogy to the ecclesiastical system and the Crusades in the twelfth and thirteenth centuries.

Dante lived in an age when these mental and spiritual habits were still strong, and yet were being subjected to conscious scrutiny. He was the most powerful critic, the most disciplined idealist of his time. At any rate, if there were others as great as he was, no record of their thoughts and aspirations has come down to us. Dante, as casual allusions in his writings show, was of course aware of and, it would seem, took for granted the current view of the

[1] A paper read to the Oxford Dante Society, 13 November 1934.

Crusade. Yet his passionate and carefully considered plea for the unity of Christian society was not, in his mind, affected by the traditional vision of an organized attack upon the enemies of Christ. He does not refer to the Crusade as the outcome of a reinvigorated Empire; indeed, when he considered the actual effects of his noble ideal of universal peace and order, he probably thought especially of the restoration of Italy. Nor was he moved, so far as we know, by the strong missionary impulses of his time. St. Thomas Aquinas, in his story of St. Francis, is made to refer to the saint's journey to Egypt:

> per la sete del martiro,
> nella presenza del Soldan superba
> predicò Cristo; (*Parad.* xi. 100–2.)

but Dante is obviously more interested in St. Francis's 'thirst for martyrdom' than in his attempt to convert the Soldan. On the other hand, the poet was deeply concerned with the fate of good men who had lived outside the Christian community.

It is clear that Dante's position claims some attention.

Life in Florence was not likely to inspire an interest in the Crusade in a precocious and observant boy. It was faction-ridden and self-absorbed. Yet Dante, at the age of eight, may have been present at one impressive scene. In the summer of 1273 Pope Gregory X—one of the great popes of history—stayed for a month in Florence on his way to the general council which he had summoned to meet at Lyons. The Greek and Latin Churches were to be united, a new emperor was to be elected, the Church was to be reformed, peace to be proclaimed, and a crusade preached. The wealthy city of Florence could not play her appropriate part so long as the Guelfs within her walls were at odds with the exiled Ghibellines without. So the Pope came, with Baldwin, the last Latin Emperor of Constantinople, now a wanderer on the face of the earth, and Charles of Anjou, the French King of Naples and Sicily. Gregory stayed in the new palace of the banking family, the Mozzi, Charles in the garden-girt house of the Frescobaldi, Baldwin in the episcopal palace over against the Baptistry. Peace was arranged, and on a hot day in July the parties gathered in the presence of Pope, three or four cardinals, and a group of archbishops and bishops. A parliament had been summoned by heralds and the ringing of bells, and the common folk gathered together in the dry bed of the Arno by the Rubaconte bridge. The emissaries of the counts and Ghibellines, and the spokesmen of the Guelfs were placed on two platforms, separated from each other. The long Latin terms of agreement were read, the parties, through their spokesmen, swore to observe the peace; and on the site of this act of reunion Pope Gregory laid the foundation-stone of a chapel, founded by his hosts the Mozzi, and dedicated to Saint Gregory the Great, whose name he had taken.[1]

Gregory passed on to his council, but in 1276 he died and the hopes of a speedy Crusade passed away with him. Eighteen years after the pacification of 1273 the last Christian stronghold in Syria fell, and all Europe was thrilled and disturbed by the news. The pope of that day, Nicholas IV, begged for aid and advice from the dioceses of the west; but in this year, 1291, Dante, now 26 years of age, was mourning the loss of Beatrice, who had died in the previous year. He would not give many thoughts to the loss of Acre.

The Florentines took a cool, business-like interest in the Holy Land. Pope Gregory's biographer, referring to the choice of Lyons as the seat of the general council, says that the people of Syria did not look favourably upon Rome or any place in Italy, for they feared that, if the council were summoned in Italy, help would come only from Lombardy, Tuscany, and Apulia, 'and they had little trust in *their* aid'. There was a brotherhood of pilgrims in Florence, and in the wills of the period money was frequently left *in subsidio terre sancte*; but the proviso is generally added, 'when there is a *passagium generale*', and occasionally a stipulation is made that the legacy is to be used for a different purpose if the Crusade should not start within three years. As Davidsohn remarks, the Florentines showed calculating foresight in matters of the soul as well as in other things.[2] Dante, as a

[1] R. Davidsohn, *Geschichte von Florenz*, II. ii. 90–3; also his *Forschungen*, iv. 211 ff.

[2] *Geschichte von Florenz*, IV. iii. 80–2, and Anmerkungen, p. 19.

citizen of Florence, was not often reminded of the Crusade. If he had habitually attended the discourses of popular preachers, he would doubtless have heard more about it, but it is not very easy to think of him as a devotee of this kind.

At the same time, the idea of the Crusade was so deeply engrained in the experience of western Christendom that an orthodox man would not lightly reject it. In fact Dante, in the *Paradiso*, implicitly appropriates the conception of the Holy War and identifies his thoughts with the justification of the Crusade. In the traditional exegesis Rahab the harlot and her household were the type of the Church; they were saved in Jericho, for Rahab's sins were remitted by her reception of Joshua's spies. The scarlet thread which she bound in her window, and which was to be the sign of her exemption from destruction, represented the blood of Christ shed for the remission of sins. Finally, by her marriage with Salmon she became the ancestress of our Lord. This characteristic piece of medieval thought, with its mingling of fact and symbolism, illustrates two ideas which sanctioned the Crusade: the devotion to the Holy Land, and the belief, as a matter of course, that any actions which led to its capture and retention were not merely justified but were *ipso facto* good and right. 'In like manner, was not Rahab the harlot justified by works, in that she received the messengers and sent them out another way?'[1] Dante appropriates everything that had been built upon this text, and goes farther still. Folquet of Marseilles, the amorous troubadour who turned Cistercian, persecuted the heretics, and during the Albigensian Crusades was bishop of Toulouse, points out Rahab to Dante in the Heaven of Venus: within that sparkling light *si tranquilla Raab*—she is at peace (*Parad.* ix. 115). The first soul to be released by Christ from Limbo, she is a trophy of His victory,

> perch'ella favorò la prima gloria
> di Josuè in sulla Terra Santa,
> che poco tocca al papa la memoria. (ll. 124–7.)

She was able, in other words, to understand the significance of Joshua's task. The Promised Land was to be the Holy

[1] James ii. 25.

Land, now unheeded by the Pope. For, Folquet goes on, the florins of Dante's native city, founded by the devil, have demoralized the Church. The sheep are scattered, for the shepherd has become a wolf:

> il maledetto fiore
> ch'ha disviate le pecore e gli agni,
> perocchè fatto ha lupo del pastore. (ll. 130–2.)

The Gospel and the Doctors of the Church—those authorities, we may observe, in which the story of Rahab is explained—are neglected. Pope and cardinals are intent upon their law books. They have no thoughts for Nazareth:

> non vanno i lor pensieri a Nazzarette,
> là dove Gabriello aperse l'ali. (ll. 137–8.)

When Dante comes to describe the Heaven of Mars, the crusading *motif* predominates. His guide here is his ancestor, Cacciaguida, who, like a runnel of light, leaves the great cross formed by the bright chanting spirits of the warriors of Christ. In the *Convivio* (ii. 14) the Heaven of Mars is compared to Music, partly because of its central position, partly because it affects meteoric bodies as harmony affects the souls of men. Here, I think, we can see a mystical expression of the function of force in the life of an organized community. Force maintains the due proportion of the elements in society, and the exercise of it thrills men with a sense of rhythmic purpose, bringing a harmony into their efforts of offence and defence. This analogy, however, is not mentioned in the *Paradiso*; perhaps Dante had outgrown it. Cacciaguida's part is three-fold: as a citizen of the old Florence he draws a gloomy contrast between the city of his day and the city of Dante's day, the one so frugal and disciplined, the other so unfit for high enterprise. As Dante's great-great-grandfather, he describes the future career of his descendant. As a crusader, he points out the souls of the great *spiriti militanti*, Joshua, Judas Maccabeus, Charlemagne, William of Orange and his converted brother-in-law, the Saracen Renouard (Rinoardo),[1] Godfrey of Bouillon, the hero of the first Crusade, and Robert

[1] See Bédier, *Les légendes épiques* (Paris, 1908), i. 92–136. The chansons relating to Renouard have not all been edited.

Guiscard. Dante was intensely proud of his ancestor and believed that he died on the second Crusade, the great expedition which St. Bernard had preached, in the army of the Emperor Conrad III, who had knighted him. Later members of Dante's family, although they confused Conrad III with Conrad II, obviously thought that Cacciaguida had died in South Italy in the expedition undertaken by Conrad II against the Saracens there ; a view probably suggested by the explicit statement of Villani that Conrad II knighted several Florentines on his way through the city.[1] But, as Cacciaguida was alive in the reign of Conrad III (1138–52) he could not possibly have been alive a century earlier, in the reign of Conrad II (1024–39). However, the important thing is not so much whether Cacciaguida fought with Conrad II or Conrad III, as how Dante regarded his ancestor's action. The words of Cacciaguida are significant ; after referring to his knighting by the emperor, he goes on :

> Dietro gli andai incontro alla nequizia
> di quella legge, il cui popolo usurpa,
> per colpa dei pastor, vostra giustizia.
> Quivi fu'io da quella gente turpa
> disviluppato dal mondo fallace,
> il cui amor molte anime deturpa,
> E venni dal martirio a questa pace. (*Parad.* xv.142–8.)[2]

He had marched against an infamy, the law of a people which had usurped what rightly belonged to Christians, and this was due to the negligence of the shepherds of Christ's sheep. His death was a martyrdom ending in the peace of heaven. Family pride brought the fate of Cacciaguida home to Dante's mind, and in a few lines he distilled, in

[1] See Paget Toynbee, *A Dictionary of Proper Names and Notable Matters in the Works of Dante*, s.v. Currado. Two of Cacciaguida's sons, so described, were alive in 1189 : ibid. s.v. Cacciaguida.

[2]
> With him did I this false religion fight
> whose people, by your shepherds' fault, the place
> have long usurped which should be yours by right.
> There was I at the hands of that foul race
> dismantled of the world's deceitful shows,
> the loss of which doth many a soul debase ;
> And came from martyrdom to this repose. (G. L. Bickersteth.)

The translation does not convey the full significance of the terms used by Dante. Probably no translation could.

his inimitable way, the whole idealism of the Crusades, as he did nowhere else. The important words are *nequizia*, *legge*, *giustizia*, *martirio*. Mohammed, *Macometto cieco* as he describes him in one of his *canzoni* to the people of Florence, was the arch-schismatic, who with his son-in-law, Ali, was placed by the poet in the eighth circle of Hell, Malebolge, as a sower of discord (*Inf.* xxviii). The charge against him and the 'foul folk' who followed him was not that he was a non-Christian, but that, knowing something of the Christian revelation, he had organized resistance and set up a rival *law*, another way of life. He had broken the harmony of the universe and this could only be restored by his and the law's destruction. The fundamental condition of harmony was justice, a word which carried with it far more significance than it does to us, and by a natural symbolism the possession of the Holy Places by the schismatics was in itself an act of injustice. Jerusalem in Dante's cosmography was the centre of the earth. Any one who died in resistance to the law of Mohammed was a martyr, and in his fighting he was sure of plenary indulgence, for he was engaged in a Holy War for a Holy Land, in defence of essential justice. This was the thought of St. Bernard, who, probably more than any other great teacher of the Christian society, influenced the moral and spiritual life of Dante.

The other references made by Dante to the Saracens and to the war against them are of a more casual kind and are easily intelligible in the light of the passages which I have analysed. When he wishes, in his epistles, to emphasize the sorry state of Italy, he says that her condition deserves the compassion of the Saracens: *nunc miseranda Italia etiam Saracenis* (*Ep.* v. 2), or stirs their ridicule: *impietatis fautores, Judaei, Saraceni et gentes sabbata nostra rident*, *et*, *ut fertur*, *conclamant*, '*Ubi est deus eorum?*' (ibid., viii. 3). When he wishes to blame the Florentine women he says that the Saracen women are more modest than they are (*Purg.* xxiii. 103). When he bursts out against the bestial, vile, and foolish doctrine of those who deny the immortality of the soul, he marshals against it the faith of all who admit the claims of reason: Aristotle, Cicero, the poets of the Gentiles, and every code of life, Jewish, Saracen, Tartar (*Conv.* ii. 9).

And in the famous and terrible diatribe against Pope Boniface VIII, celebrating, in the year to which Dante ascribes his vision, the first great Jubilee at Rome, he taunts him with a perversion of the very idea of the Crusade:

> Lo principe de' nuovi Farisei,
> avendo guerra presso a Laterano,
> e non con Saracin, nè con Giudei,
> chè ciascun suo nimico era Cristiano,
> e nessuno era stato a vincer Acri,
> nè mercatante in terra di Soldano. (*Inf.* xxvii. 85–91.)[1]

The point here is that Pope Boniface had preached a Crusade even against members of the Sacred College of Cardinals; and that in the great bull of indulgence to those who visited the shrines of St. Peter and St. Paul during the year of Jubilee, he had expressly excepted, together with the merchants who traded with the Saracens (who were mentioned by Dante), those in rebellion against the Church. In another bull he defined these as Frederick of Aragon and his Sicilian subjects and whoever should receive the Colonna.

A movement which lasts for over two hundred years necessarily changes its character. It tends to harden or to be adjusted to the changes in social life. The Crusades began in a mystical mood and, although they were organized locally, were not acts of state. The crusader was a volunteer carried away by enthusiasm. In course of time the assumption of the cross became a form of penance or the means of getting rid of a troublesome subject or neighbour. Thus in 1282 King Edward I undertook to provide honourably for David, the brother of Llywelyn of Wales, if he would take the cross, provided that he did not return *nisi per regiam clementiam*; to which suggestion the hot-blooded Welshman replied that when he wished to go to the Holy Land he would go voluntarily and *ex voto*, for God, not for man; God grant that he never make an unwilling pilgrimage, for forced service is unpleasing to God. And if he should be stirred

[1] 'The Prince of the new Pharisees—waging war near to the Lateran, and not with Saracens or Jews; for every enemy of his was Christian, and none had been to conquer Acre, nor been a merchant in the Soldan's land.' (P. H. Wicksteed.)

up to go by his own will, he would deserve reward, not the disinheritance which the king had in mind.[1] The Holy Land was so far away, the danger from the infidel, after he had been finally checked in Spain, was so unrelated to the everyday life of the west, the chances of a safe return were so remote, that religious enthusiasm, and religious enthusiasm alone, could have given impetus to the Crusade. It is probable that Pope Urban II, when he preached the first Crusade in 1095, was influenced especially by monastic feeling, voiced by the abbey of Cluny, and the Crusade was sustained throughout by the strange apocalyptic spiritualism which we find in the monastic outlook on society. In the versions which have come down to us of Pope Urban's great sermon at Clermont we can see all the elements of this view of history, so different from the political theory of the schools and the doctrines of feudal rights and duties. He cries for vengeance on those who have profaned Jerusalem and maltreated the servants of Christ. He appeals to the memory of Charlemagne and his paladins. He pictures the violated state of the Holy Sepulchre, and calls for volunteers to seize back the Holy Land. God gave this land to his children—here we have the Joshua and Rahab *motif*—Jerusalem is the centre of the earth, a second paradise; Jerusalem is sanctified and glorified by the birth, the life, the sufferings, the death and burial of the Saviour, is His for all time, and yet it is now in the hands of impious strangers. St. Bernard, fifty years later, made this idea the centre of his exhortations. Men of good will, who have purified their lives and are ready to die in battle for the Holy Places, have solved the soldiers' dilemma; they have purged their warfare of the sin and rapine which are inseparable from it in the normal fighting on earth. They are cleansed of the stain of the shedder of blood. This is the burden of his tract addresses to the Templars. Crude warriors, as we learn from the best chronicle of the first Crusade, could not understand defeat in such a cause. They felt that God had betrayed them. But the preachers and moralists had their answer. Those who die are martyrs. God has willed it so, for He wishes to take such to Him-

[1] *Registrum Epistolarum J. Peckham* (Rolls Series), ii. 467, 471.

self. To the end the songs of the crusaders—many of which survive—are full of this outlook on life—of passionate longing for home, of hatred and contempt for the slack or worldly-wise, and of exultation in their own self-sacrifice.[1] Yet, while this spirit continued to sustain the Crusades, circumstances changed their character or modified the outlook of cool-headed men. And this in two ways.

(i) The experience of the first Crusade convinced all men of influence, including the zealots, that the expeditions must be carefully organized. St. Bernard himself gave warning, and a later writer, who may have been Stephen Langton, summed up the danger in a few pregnant sentences: 'Christian men should not tempt God and start war, headlong and proudly, few against many, because they have a good Lord and a mighty. For God wishes his servants so to trust in Him that they be not reckless and negligent to work wisely.' Richard I organized his crusade with much care. The result was that, although leadership lay with the Pope and the financial arrangements were in his hands, the Crusades tended to have a national basis, and to be subject to political considerations. Moreover, the establishment of the Latin states in the East and the uneasy relations both of them and of the Papacy with the Eastern Empire emphasized the feudal character of the movement and its connexion with general problems of state. Just as it was not everybody's duty to go, so the decision to embark upon a Crusade was a matter to be carefully weighed in the light of the calls upon the resources and attention of popes and princes. There are cases in which a local bishop, at the request of his lay suzerain, excommunicated an ardent crusader who insisted on going to the East against the will of his lord; while the delays in papal initiative, rather conventionally deplored by Dante, became as a matter of course an occasion of scandal to zealots and visionaries. Finally, the disunion of Europe and notably the internecine war between the Papacy and an emperor who was regarded as a heretic and schismatic, dislocated the whole system. Just because the organization of the Holy War became so systematic, it was inevitably adapted

[1] J. Bédier and P. Aubry, *Les chansons de Croisade* (Paris, 1909).

to other purposes. The Holy War became an instrument to be turned against heresy and enemies of the Church within the borders of Christendom. Historically, the right to use force within the Christian society against heretics was centuries older than the Crusades. It was described in the law books of the Church and was derived from the writings of St. Augustine. But the Crusades provided both a model and a means for its operation. The Crusades became ineffective not because men lost interest in them but because they were too interested in extending their range. Religious passion was directed against itself, and in the course of the conflict the natural leader of a great crusading movement, the emperor, lost ground. It is impossible to exaggerate the embarrassment which was caused by the spectacle of an excommunicated emperor fighting for his existence against his spiritual ally. In a charming illustrative manuscript of the famous German law book, the *Sachsenspiegel*, pope and emperor are portrayed sitting side by side with their arms round each other's necks. But this idealism lost all reality as the thirteenth century proceeded. The apocalyptic writers themselves were divided against each other: to some the emperor had ceased to be the protector of public law and order, and the name Rome, the symbol of secular imperial power, was synonymous with the name Babylon. To others a time was at hand when Teutons and Spaniards would combine to crush the French and rule the earth. This embarrassment can be seen very clearly in Dante's time after the fall of Acre, for example in the fumbling proposals made by the clergy of the diocese of Norwich to a church council in London. In their eyes the emperor was the natural leader in the task of recovery, but he seemed so unlikely. Hence the Crusade became, not a call to unity and peace, in the preparation of Christian endeavour, but a means of national ambition. Peace and unity indeed, but to be attained by this ruler or that as part of a great national venture. In his tract on the recovery of the Holy Land the French legist Pierre Dubois (*c.* 1306) makes the Crusade the object of a Europe reorganized under French guidance. The Church is to be disendowed and its ministers salaried; military, financial, and educational systems are to be devised in order to make success sure; the Mediterranean is to be a French lake; and the French king is to direct operations from a safe place in the rear. Dante wrote his *Monarchia* in this troubled world. His nearer vision was confined to the chaos in Italy, his distant vision pierced through all the fantasies of his time in an effort to see and justify the real unity and order, grounded in history and the nature of things, safe from the sophistries of papal lawyers and apologists. He had no time to give to the Crusade. If he ever thought of it, he felt that it must wait till Christendom was saved from itself. The champions of the Holy Places were unclean.

(ii) The second change to which I wish to refer was the outcome of criticism and observation; it might be described as an expression of the scientific spirit, unmoved by the hyperbole of the zealots. The traditional, probably the official, view was that the Christian community was in a state of natural and perpetual war against the infidel. This view is expressed by the great canon lawyer Hostiensis. But as the thirteenth century goes on we can trace a modification in this attitude. The 'Roman war', as Hostiensis described it, is not always just. The infidel has rights; he is justiciable and can hold property. St. Thomas Aquinas distinguished between the heretic, who has no rights, for he has broken his oath to the society in which he lives, and the infidel. Those who have never believed, the Jews and Gentiles, cannot be forced to believe, and war should only be made on them in order to prevent the persecution of Christians.[1] In other words, the Crusades were defensive. The distinction made by St. Thomas provided the grounds for the expansion of missions which characterizes the late thirteenth century and the early fourteenth century: the work of the Franciscans, the experiments of the Catalan Ramon Lull, the foundation of chairs of Hebrew and Arabic in the Dominican schools, and the like. It also reveals a new attitude to the infidel which the missions helped to strengthen, an attitude which Roger Bacon characteristically expressed with practical logic when he said that Crusades were a cruel and useless waste of time and

[1] H. Pissard, *La Guerre Sainte en pays chrétien* (Paris, 1912), pp. 108 ff.

that the infidel should be converted, not attacked. Through a very interesting chain of circumstances this view was assisted by the great Mongol movements in Asia. If the Tartars had maintained the energy of the invasion which brought them almost in sight of the Alps and had they been Mohammedans, as they generally became later, the danger caused by their appearance would probably have brought Europe together in the greatest of all the Crusades. This would have been a defensive war as exacting as the conflicts of the eighth century. We can read in the pages of Matthew Paris how deeply the news of the Tartar advance stirred the imagination of those in far-away England. But the danger passed. The invasions lost impetus, broke, or were diverted. The conquerors of China, Persia, and Caucasia were disposed to be curious and tolerant in religious matters, even to take sides with Christian peoples, such as the Armenians, against the Mohammedans in Egypt and Syria. Asia was open to travellers, missionaries, and merchants. The West entertained lively hopes of its conversion, through its new masters, to Christianity. Giles of Rome, for example, made a catechism for Tartars. Hence the changes in Asia helped to extend the horizon of the western mind, to instil into the theological conception of the Crusade—as later in Africa—the spirit of adventure and curiosity. Roger Bacon himself provides a good illustration of this modification of feeling. Although he did not believe in the Crusades, Bacon was greatly influenced by contemporary apocalyptic. He was sure that Antichrist was coming and, in his practical way, he thought that something should be done about it. He did not exult in the cataclysm as an inevitable stage in the passage to a new age of an angel king or angel pope, nor did he try to identify Antichrist with any existing power in west or east. Antichrist would break through the Caspian Gates, and it would be well if the Pope would organize research into all the magical arts which the enemy would employ and prepare Christendom to meet him. Instead of concentrating on these devices—burning glasses, flying machines, self-propelled engines of war (in other words, wireless, poison gas, aeroplanes, and tanks)—learned men, doubtless instigated by the devil, were, says Bacon, absorbed in trivialities. Yet Bacon refused to believe that the Tartars, who had broken through the Caspian Gates, gave a clue to the coming of Antichrist; that kind of invasion had happened too often. Now this interesting argument suggests that men were ceasing to identify the terrible and catastrophic with anything which could become familiar. They were gradually becoming aware of the size of the world and of the nature of immediate dangers. The apocalyptic mood was giving way before the spirit of research; and the inevitable Antichrist was thrust farther back into the great unknown. Men like Bacon were as credulous as their fellows, but not about things which they could investigate; they firmly believed that, if the Bible and other books were read properly, the coming of Antichrist could be calculated, and they were not prepared to sit down quietly and wait. As Mr. Little says of Bacon in another connexion—'he erects a thoroughly modern building on a thoroughly medieval foundation'. And the various views held about the infidel in the thirteenth century show how knowledge both fostered mental detachment and was fostered by it. Men have always been capable of respect for an adversary whom they have learned to know or whose greatness is impressed upon them. In order to maintain loathing and hatred he must be so remote that it is possible to make him hateful or loathsome or he must be avoided because he is loathsome and hateful. Long cherished illusion, and reasoned theological prejudice in particular, can of course keep alive a sense of loathing for a long time, even while exceptions are made in favour of individuals. One of Dante's contemporaries at Florence, a great Dominican preacher, expressed his anti-Semitism with incessant and virulent rhetoric, although he had the highest admiration for the Jew who had taught him Hebrew. Anti-Semitism and also the hatred of the infidel was grounded in Biblical exegesis, not on race prejudice. But even here we can see the gradual influence of more accurate information at work. Humbert de Romanis, for example, tried to show that the Mohammedans must perish by the sword and could not be converted, by drawing out, with fair accuracy, the incompatibility between the law of Christ and the law of Mohammed. Others were naturally more tolerant. Burchard of Mount Zion, who wrote about 1283, 'gives the beliefs of Islam accurately and concludes "they are very hospitable, courteous, and kindly"'. There are a great many instances, quite apart from the daily experience of those who lived among the Saracens in the Holy Land.[1]

Dante never moved among Saracens. He had imbibed the traditional theology about the Holy Places and the war against the infidel. He had no opportunity, and probably no desire, to know more about them; but he was not indiscriminate in his outlook, as his judgements on Averroës and Siger of Brabant show. And at least once he shows that his proud imagination had been made captive. In the *Convivio* (iv. 11) Saladin's name appears casually in a list of the munificent. And Saladin is found in Limbo, with the famous men and women of the ancient world. He is mentioned alongside Brutus and Aristotle:

> Vidi quel Bruto che cacciò Tarquino,
> Lucrezia, Julia, Marzia e Corniglia,
> *e solo in parte vidi il Saladino.*
>
> Poi che innalzai un poco più le ciglia,
> vidi il maestro di color che sanno,
> seder tra filosofica famiglia. (*Inf.* iv. 127–32.)[2]

A perplexing problem naturally emerges at this point, a problem which, as the more profound critics of Dante have seen, raises the whole issue of the relation between the poet's independent insight and his dependence upon orthodox tradition and the great teachers of the Church. I refer to the reconciliation of the Divine wisdom and mercy with the fate of the damned who had not brought their damnation upon themselves. Dante's mind was not

[1] See D. C. Munro, 'The Western Attitude towards Islam during the Crusades', in *Speculum* (1931), vi, 329–44. From the first this indulgent attitude, though liable to interruption by religious feeling, was prevalent on both sides in Syria and the Holy Land.

[2] 'I saw that Brutus who expelled the Tarquin, Lucretia, Julia, Martia, and Cornelia; and, by himself apart, I saw the Saladin. When I raised my eyelids a little higher, I saw the Master of those that know, sitting amid a philosophic family.' (P. H. Wicksteed.)

satisfied by a stark division between Christians and non-Christians, and in this he was in line with earlier moralists like Otto of Freising who had developed the doctrine of the Two Cities of good and evil, whose inhabitants are mingled within the Church Militant. He believed that there would be surprises hereafter when the elect were known. And yet God had ordained the grouping of men in Church and Empire as necessary avenues to Paradise. Scholars, like Fritz Kern and Karl Vossler, who argue that Dante transcended the teaching of the *Monarchia* and found a mystical and moral solution of the dilemma rather than satisfaction in theological explanations, are probably right. However this may be, this dilemma is the main theme of the cantos devoted to the Heaven of Jupiter, the revelation of the just (*Parad.* xviii–xx).

O perpetui fiori
dell'eterna letizia, che pur uno
parer mi fate tutti i vostri odori,

solvetemi spirando il gran digiuno
che lungamente m'ha tenuto in fame. (xix. 22–6.)

Un uom nasce alla riva
dell'Indo, e quivi non è chi ragioni
di Cristo, nè chi legga, nè chi scriva;

e tutti i suoi voleri ed atti buoni
sono, quanto ragione umana vede,
senza peccato in vita o in sermoni.

More non battezzato e senza fede;
ov'è questa giustizia che il condanna?
ov'è la colpa sua, se ei non crede? (xix. 70–8.)

And, again, after the sight of Trajan and Ripheus:

E voi, mortali, tenetevi stretti
a giudicar; chè noi, che Dio vedemo,
non conosciamo ancor tutti gli eletti;

ed enne dolce così fatto scemo,
perchè il ben nostro in questo ben s'affina,
chè quel che vuole Iddio e noi volemo. (xx. 133–8.)[1]

[1] See opposite.

Dante did not cease to be a man of the thirteenth century when he wrote these lines. Spiritual pain leading to serene acquiescence was the core of genuine religious experience in the Middle Ages. An informed ignorance, a faith which has beaten its wings against the limits of the knowable—these are not new. But no man faced more boldly the dilemma which lies in wait for the orthodox Christian who tries to plumb the depths of divine justice.

[1] Then cried I: 'O perpetual flowers, aflame
with the eternal joy, who to my sense
cause all your perfumes to appear the same,
break with your breath the stubborn abstinence,
which, finding no relief on earth, hath held
my hungry spirit in such long suspense.'...

'For thou wouldst say: "A man first sees the light
beside the Indus, where is none who could
discourse of Christ or read of him or write;
all his volitions and his acts are good,
so far as human reason sees, nor fail
in life or speech, of perfect rectitude.
He dies unchristened and an infidel:
where is this justice that condemns the man?
where, if without faith, is he culpable?"'...

'Judge, then, you mortals, with restraint; for we,
to whom the sight of God is granted, still
know not how many the elect shall be;
and us this very task with joy doth fill,
because we find our crowning good herein,
that what is willed by God we also will.'

(G. L. Bickersteth.)

III

POPE BONIFACE VIII[1]

BISHOP CREIGHTON entitled his book *A History of the Papacy from the Great Schism to the Sack of Rome*. He prefixed two introductory chapters, the one on the rise of the papal power, the other on the popes at Avignon. As he read its history, the papacy dominated Europe for rather more than two centuries. Pope Gregory VII revealed it, in all its strength, after a long period of preparation. Pope Boniface VIII, in spite of his high assertion of its pretensions, disclosed its weakness. 'The suddenness and abruptness of the calamity which befell Boniface impressed' the fate of the papal power 'indelibly on the minds of men. The papacy had first shown its power by a great dramatic act; its decline was manifested in the same way. The drama of Anagni is to be set against the drama of Canossa'. The disgraceful captivity of later popes in Avignon, the still more disgraceful schism, the efforts of the Church in the Conciliar movement to find a way to a corporate reconstruction, the re-establishment of an Italian papacy which maintained its local power by a system of concordats with European princes, finally the Reformation and the division of Italy into spheres of interest between great Catholic powers, followed naturally, if not inevitably, from the collapse revealed to the world on the morrow of the great jubilee of the year 1300. The drama of Anagni in 1303 stands half-way in history between the humiliation of the emperor Henry IV by Pope Gregory VII and the sack of Rome by the soldiers of the emperor Charles V. It divides, both in time and in the logic of human affairs, the story of the later, the real, Middle Ages.

Fifty years have gone by since Creighton, in 1882, published the first two volumes of his history from his college living in Northumberland. He lived in a good place in a district not devoid of inspiration for a spacious survey of

[1] This paper was delivered as the Creighton Lecture in the University of London in November 1932. It is here printed in a slightly revised form, with some references to the work on *Boniface VIII*, by T. S. R. Boase, since published.

the strange movement of ecclesiastical history, of the chaotic incidents of Italian politics. Bede had looked out over the past from this northern country twelve hundred years before; in the same country in Creighton's own time, Thomas Hodgkin was writing the story of the Invaders of Italy. One of the most illustrious of the contemporaries of Boniface VIII, Duns Scotus, was in Creighton's time believed to have been born in Creighton's own parish and to have been a fellow of Creighton's own college at Oxford.[1] We may still salute, with admiration and respect, Creighton's great book, so clear and vivid, with its easy mastery of detail and its broad sweep and humane common sense. It has those qualities which we may well envy in these days, for they belong to the leisurely achievement of ripe and vigorous minds, working in quiet places.

Yet fifty years are fifty years, and this particular half-century has seen more intense activity spent upon the problems of medieval history, notably, perhaps, in the age of Dante and Boniface VIII, than in all previous centuries. Does Creighton's judgement still stand? The answer is Yes and No. That the last years of the thirteenth century, when the Crusades came to an end, and French and Spanish powers were established in the Mediterranean, were a turning-point in European history, is realized now better than it has ever been realized before. That papal power in the fourteenth century was a different thing from the power of Gregory VII or Innocent III is a commonplace of accepted history. At the same time, our conception of the process of transition from one stage of history to the other has been greatly enriched. The emphasis is different from that suggested by the clear-cut generalizations and the dramatic moments upon which historians insisted fifty years ago. Conventional judgements, if they do not ring false, fall like thin and twittering cries upon the ear, as the crowded scenes, the incessant variety of purpose, opinion and passion, amidst which Pope Boniface had to make himself felt, are revealed to us. And the Pope himself falls into place, as he ceases to

[1] He is now known to have been born at Maxton near Roxburgh, and to have been the son of Ninian Duns of Littledean. See A. G. Little in the *English Hist. Rev.* (1932), xlvii. 569, and the references there given.

move before us like a buskined figure of tragedy and becomes a man. In this paper I am concerned with some aspects of this rich variety, rather than with the ghostly refinements of reflection which we call the verdict of history.

Few episodes in medieval history are better known than the brief pontificate of Pope Celestine V in the year 1294. After violent quarrels at Rome, the Sacred College, by this time reduced to an oligarchy of eleven cardinals, had gathered together, in October 1293, at Perugia. The cardinals sat in conclave for nine months, unable to agree. Twenty years before, in the Council of Lyons, Pope Gregory X had issued a stiff decree on the procedure in papal elections, but a later pope had abrogated it, and now for the last time the cardinals were able to wrangle and delay at their pleasure. An attempt made by King Charles of Naples to share and direct their deliberations was firmly resisted by the cardinal who was soon to become Pope Boniface VIII. At last, partly from weariness, partly through the more informal and secretive manipulations of King Charles, the electors were reduced to a mood susceptible to inspiration. The old cardinal of Ostia had been much impressed by the visions of coming disaster seen in this disgraceful period of delay by a holy hermit. Why not end the disgrace and all disputes by the election of the hermit? A common enthusiasm united the college: some had long been affected by the spiritual movements then so widespread in Italy, others were tired of the fierce family ambitions and the political considerations which divided them. So, early in July 1294, Peter of Murrone was elected.[1] At the news a wave of astonishment and awe, mingled with the exultation of the spirituals, passed through the countryside. The feelings of amusement or misgiving which some must have had were hidden. The cardinals sent ambassadors across the borders of the kingdom of Naples to the hills of the Abruzzi. They made the ascent of Mount Murrone and sought the recluse. They found him in a cave, an emaciated, blear-eyed, unkempt prophet. Kings, nobles, ecclesiastics, votaries had gathered there. Peter left his retreat in the company of

[1] Not, as is usually supposed, in an act of sudden inspiration, but gradually, on the 5 July and following days: Boase, op. cit., p. 41.

Charles of Naples and his son, the titular king of Hungary. In Aquila, on the northern edge of the kingdom, he was crowned pope as Celestine V. But he never entered the Papal States. The cardinals had to come to him. King Charles had no mind to surrender his precious charge and the Pope was brought by slow stages to Naples. There he held his court in the royal stronghold, the Castel Nuovo. The poor old man stood the strain for six or seven weeks. In surroundings strange and alien to him, he, the lord of the world, was the helpless victim of those about him. Ignorant of the intricacies of papal business, too old and dreamy to shape a resolute policy, he longed for solitude. After taking anxious counsel, he appeared on 13 December before the cardinals and resigned his task. 'You are running away', said Cardinal Matthew Orsini, 'from what every fool and every wise man longs to have.' Celestine V had done at least one service to the papacy. He restored the disciplinary regulations of Pope Gregory X about the conduct of papal elections. Within a fortnight after his resignation, on the third scrutiny, Cardinal Benedict Caetani was elected pope. A month later, on 23 January 1295, he was consecrated and crowned as Boniface VIII in Rome.

Had Peter of Murrone been merely an obscure solitary, his elevation and retirement would have been but a curious incident in papal history. But he was much more than this. Thirty years before, this uncouth but ardent plebeian had founded an order, known after his pontificate as the Celestine, whose houses were scattered about central and southern Italy; and although he had divested himself, like St. Francis, of all authority over his order and had gone back to his cave on Mount Murrone, he was revered both as its founder and as a saintly man endowed with the gift of prophecy. His election raised the highest hopes in circles far beyond his order. It was welcomed as the fulfilment of the dreams of Joachim of Fiore and St. Francis. The Spiritual Franciscans, whose anxieties were voiced by their poet, Jacopone da Todi, waited in breathless expectation. Would he hold his own? Would he, remote from all party and faction, be the father of all as he had been the father of his brethren? Would he be strong enough to realize on the throne of St. Peter the visions which had come to him in his quiet cell? When he recognized the right of the scattered and persecuted little groups which claimed to be the true Franciscans to live as they willed or to join themselves to his own order, they saw the dawn of the new age. Then came the bewilderment, the bitterness, of the great refusal, soon to be followed by passionate concern for the fate of the master. For Celestine had not been allowed to go back to his own people. His existence was embarrassing enough to the new pope; as the centre, however unwilling, of a fanatical party, and the gathering point of every hostile element, he might be a public danger. He was brought northwards. He eluded his companions and tried to escape. He was found and brought to a cell, like his old cell in Abruzzi, in the castle of Fumone, near the papal city of Anagni. There, in May 1296, he died. Pope Boniface was to find that he was more dangerous dead than alive. Celestine pursued him through the troubles of his reign and tormented his memory after he had joined him in death. Celestine, the story ran, had been harried by his ambitious rival into retirement. The resignation, the work of fraud, was invalid, and Boniface was no true pope. And later, so the legend grew, Celestine had not died a natural death. The new pope had driven a nail into his head. Even his canonization by Pope Clement V ten years after the death of Boniface was a move in the vendetta against the memory of Boniface carried on by his implacable enemies. The political and personal enemies of Boniface joined mystics and enthusiasts in exalting the one pope and defaming the other. When Celestine was elected, Dante, a young man of twenty-nine, was living in Florence, towards the end of those happy years to which the Florentines looked back as the halcyon days of the Republic. When Boniface died, Dante, a casual victim of papal policy, was an exile in Verona. The poet, if the usual identification of him who made the great refusal can be accepted, put Celestine in the vestibule of Hell among those who are neither dead nor alive; to Boniface, his great enemy, he gave a place much lower down, among the simoniacs.

The contrast between the two popes has been the theme of disputants and historians from their time to this. Any serious estimate of Boniface and his pontificate must, indeed, be an elaboration of this theme. In the rest of this paper I shall first try to explain the position as he found it and to describe how he faced the problems of his day. Then I shall say more about Boniface himself.

'Henceforth', wrote Creighton, 'it was clear that the papacy had become a great political institution: its spiritual significance had been merged in its worldly importance. It needed a statesman to baffle princes by his astuteness, not a saint to kindle by his holiness spiritual aspirations among the masses.' Like most clear-cut judgements, the words give only half the truth. They set aside the 'spiritual significance' of the papal system which Boniface accepted as a matter of course; they neglect the practical difficulties which no pope, however great a saint he might be, could hope to escape. For during the thirteenth century the Church, as it surmounted one crisis after another, heard the voice of

> a subtler Sphinx renew
> Riddles of death Thebes never knew.

At one time the Church, in the uneasy impulse to realize its own ideals, had found relief in the movements of monastic reformation. But for rude peoples gradually finding their way in the troublesome, if self-imposed, task of civilization, these were an uncertain means of inspiration. The great process of discipline which culminated in the days of Pope Gregory VII was more consistent with the traditions of Constantine, of Ambrose and Augustine, of Pope Gregory and of Charles the Great. It absorbed and directed the monastic revivals, and strove after an independent episcopate, looking to Rome for guidance, a celibate clergy, a common body of law, a clear-cut yet adaptable penitential system, sound and coherent teaching about the sacraments, above all about the Mass, in which the Church daily renewed its life. In the eyes of the great saints, thinkers, and administrators who, during the next two centuries, enriched the Church, the body of doctrine and practice which developed was an organic whole. Whether they strove like St. Bernard and Grosseteste for its amendment, or tried to understand and explain it, as in their different ways Abelard or Hugh of St. Victor or the great scholastics tried, or worked for it like St. Thomas Becket and Pope Innocent III, they never questioned its validity. They did not regard the articulated system of government, however defective, as separable from the deposit of thought and experience, however inscrutable. In our judgement upon any vigorous pope we can never afford to forget the weight and momentum of this great heritage which it was his duty to safeguard. Nor can we impute to his critics or enemies the wisdom of the onlooker or the detachment of the sceptic. He was bound as a President of the United States is bound by the Constitution or an English Prime Minister by the traditions of parliamentary government. Pope Boniface VIII may have been unwise in his choice of the occasion of his great pronouncements, and in the uncompromising vigour of their phrasing, but he was no revolutionary seeking after an unfamiliar world.[1] The famous bull *Unam Sanctam* is one of the most carefully drafted documents which have ever emerged from the papal chancery. It is a formal exposition of the plenitude of papal power, spiritual and temporal, and was later included in the *Extravagantes communes*,[2] a collection of decretals made at the end of the fifteenth century, which became part of the *Corpus Juris Canonici*. In its emphasis upon the derivative nature of secular power—that, while part of the divine order, this has a dependent, not an independent authority—it follows the argument of Giles of Rome, the foremost apologist of the papacy. Two of its main theses are derived, through Giles and other writers, from a famous passage in Hugh of St. Victor and the equally famous, though much discussed, treatment by St. Bernard of the doctrine of the two swords. In the same year, 1302, in which the bull was issued, the same high claims were admitted in formal terms by the chancellor of Albert of Austria, the emperor-elect.

Anti-papal propaganda, especially in France, had pro-

[1] Cf. the judgement of Mr. Boase: 'Boniface had no new vision for his generation. He sought the climax of the existing system, and examined its details with skill and throughness, exploring their possibilities. But he had no inspiration to make anew. His way was along the beaten track, however grandly he took it' (op. cit., p. 112).

[2] Book I, tit. viii. c. 1.

voked Boniface. But drastic doctrine in politics has often, perhaps always, been made possible by opposition. The doctrines of parliamentary sovereignty and of the divine right of kings were forged from pliable materials in the heat of controversy. The point is that in the eyes of the papalists who looked over Europe about the year 1300, the position of *Unam Sanctam*, if the precious heritage from the past was to be maintained, was the only position to take, and, if logic was to be the order of the day, had its rational and natural roots in the experience of the Church. Apart from tradition and the logic of experience, doctrines such as these come easily, in our own day no less than in the past, to impatient minds, who seem to see all that they stand for endangered by fatuity or reaction. Let us imagine a Boniface or a Giles of Rome arguing as follows:

> The Church acknowledges no more than a conditional loyalty to any established government or authority. It seeks its ends irrespective of the numbers of its supporters. Governments must be judged and dealt with according to their respect for the broad ends of the Church. . . . Governments which act according to the standards of the Church are to be supported and served, and those that do not do so are to be opposed with all the energy the Church can bring to the task, and in every possible way that the situation renders advisable. The support of government is subject to the condition that the acts of government be themselves reasonable and legal and that the Law respect the prior claims of the common welfare of humanity. This denial to governments of any absolute rights is a fundamental article with the Church.

I am inclined to think that these sentences would have seemed rather crude to the medieval canonist. They lack precision and balance, although they show the right spirit. With the substitution of the word 'Church' for the words 'X society', they are taken from a recent manifesto on behalf of a reformed international Liberal party, and were written by Mr. H. G. Wells.

The view that the secular is subject to the spiritual power had hardened during the half-century which separated Boniface VIII from the great pope Innocent IV, the first pope to give unequivocal expression to it. Hitherto the prevalent doctrine had been that of the harmonious co-operation, each in its own sphere, of the two powers. As the classic exposition of it by Dante shows, the doctrine of harmony was by no means dead. It was to have importance in later history. But the implacable quarrel between the papacy and the Hohenstaufen emperors had forced the issue of sovereignty. Of two irreconcilable powers, one must be the greater, the sovereign. Pope Boniface took the same view in the face of states which, as they became more firmly knit, more conscious of their unity and of their past, maintained a doctrine of sovereignty of their own. Both Philip the Fair of France and Edward I of England were ready, if pressed, to claim the right of their kingdoms to control their own destinies and to define the secular duties of their own clergy. The king of France, protector of the Church, had, it was argued, no temporal superior. His rights went back to a time when there was no papal power. And Edward, when he repelled Boniface's intervention on behalf of Scotland, pointed to the conquest of the British Isles by Brutus the Trojan, and to the subjection of Albanactus, the youngest son of Brutus, to Locrinus the eldest. In short the appeal to history and the assertion of sovereignty were arguments which could be used by both sides, and, as each party felt the pressure of opposition, the more emphatic each became. One of Philip's legists, writing three years after Boniface's death, saw visions of a reconstructed Europe, in which the Pope and clergy would be delivered from all the trammels of worldly things, all Church property be leased in perpetuity to laymen in return for a fixed rent, and the patrimony of St. Peter be entrusted to the care of the king of France. It was a hectic return to more sober schemes of the past, when the papal system, irksome though it was, lay more lightly on the will of princes, and was less firmly entrenched in the social life of Europe.

The cause alike of this entrenchment and of the criticism

which it provoked, is to be found in the Crusades. The attempt to explain the Crusades as a social or economic development has lost something of its charm, but we are still inclined, I think, to try to explain them away as an abnormal development in medieval life, and to suppose that Europe had returned to sanity by the time of Pope Boniface. I believe on the contrary that the Holy War was a natural outcome of the reconstruction which I have sketched, that it was regarded as the function, if not the main duty, of a united Christendom, and that as a mental habit it long survived its practical importance. It was an acknowledgement of the right to use force in behalf of the service of Christ if persuasion and spiritual weapons either failed or were out of place. This teaching began to creep into the law books of the Church in the eleventh century, as part of the Hildebrandine system, and it was supported, if not actually suggested, by extracts from the writings of St. Augustine. It was accepted by earnest men and idealists of all kinds, cut across all divisions of opinion, and, in the days of Pope Boniface, was a common starting-point in minds which seemed to agree about nothing else. The political and ecclesiastical readjustment of Europe was argued in terms of the Crusade. The Crusade was the justification for the Empire in lands such as England, which would have repudiated any obligation to the Emperor.[1] Hatred and fear of the infidel had helped to inspire the teaching of Joachim of Fiore, and his indifference to the Holy War was one of the allegations brought against Boniface VIII. Even those whose thoughts had turned to the importance of persuasion, to the provision of missionary colleges for the teaching of Arabic and other eastern languages, to an evangelization of the world by personal sacrifice, found it hard to reject the conception of the Holy War. That strange indefatigable man, Ramon Lull, who poured out a stream of symbolical romances, educational tracts, and treatises on an infallible logical method, did not reject it. Fresh from his first missionary journey to Tunis, he was in Naples when Pope Celestine arrived in 1294. He hoped much from Celestine and presented him with a passionate

[1] Cf. Bartholomew Cotton, *Historia Anglicana* (Rolls Series), p. 208.

petition for the conversion of the heathen. He urged the creation of colleges and the selection of able preachers, but he urged also the need for a great crusade in those critical days when the Mongol conquerors of Asia seemed to be wavering between Christianity and Mohammedanism. After the election of Boniface Ramon pursued the new pope to Rome and had several interviews with him. This quick-minded impatient Catalan had made himself a nuisance; he was regarded as a tiresome eccentric. As he complains himself:

> I look men in the face—would tell my thought—
> But few are they that heed: the rest say naught,
> Then call me fool.[1]

But he was not rejected because he believed in the Crusade, but because, an enthusiast who had no experience of the daily responsibilities of popes and princes, he got in the way.

In fact, as was inevitable, the Crusade had got in the way of itself. Four great councils of the Church were summoned between 1215 and 1311. At all of them the programme was the pacification of Europe and legislation about outstanding questions in doctrine, discipline, reform and politics, with a view to united action in the Holy War. At two of these councils, both held at Lyons, in 1245 and 1274, intensely difficult problems, relating to the Empire and, in 1274, to the union of the Greek and Latin churches, had to be dealt with. They were issues which, with their various ramifications, form the background of the pontificate of Boniface. On each occasion clerical property was heavily taxed for the purposes of a crusade. The popes appeared as the arbiters of Europe. They assumed the responsibility for creating order and had the disposal of the crusading taxes. On this foundation the material power of the papacy in the thirteenth century was built. By canon law, generally accepted by secular rulers, the taxation of the clergy for temporal purposes was forbidden. With the acquiescence of Christendom the taxation of the clergy by the papacy for spiritual purposes, the defence and advancement of the Church, became an established fact. The

[1] E. Allison Peers, *Ramon Lull*, p. 258.

application of these revenues, in the name of order and orthodoxy, to further papal policy was the natural, and not illogical, result. That the Crusade was postponed by political difficulties was indisputable. That heresy, schism, and the self-seeking aggrandizement of princes should be put down with the aid of force and of the new papal resources was an easy deduction. The Vicar of Christ could alone decide whether the circumstances justified such action. Hence came the development of papal despotism, and the extension in all directions of the conception of the Holy War; the blurring of the distinction between heresy and opposition to the will of the Pope; the increasing resort to papal taxation and the insistence upon the immunity of the clergy from the taxation of princes, which lie behind the bull *Clericis laicos* and the first quarrel between Boniface and the kings of France and England. Hence the resistance of communities, conscious of their own unity and faced by their own complicated obligations, to a papacy whose intervention with their affairs and their wealth far transcended the activities of Gregory VII or even of Innocent III. And hence the indignation of those who, feeling that everything was wrong in a world so alien from the spirit of St. Francis, spent themselves in prophetic passion.

Such was the heritage of Pope Boniface. He entered upon it with alacrity. When he was elected at the end of 1294 he was over sixty years of age, but he was confident, vigorous and ambitious. His family, the Caetani, had long been settled in the hill town of Anagni and was closely connected with the other great families of the Campagna. He had popes and cardinals among his kindred, and after a sound training in law both at Bologna and under famous masters he had found a congenial career in the service of the papal court. During busy years of activity as cardinal and papal legate he had become familiar with affairs, and he must have watched the fumbling of his short-lived predecessors with impatience. The last great pope, Gregory X, who had brought together in a brief union the Greek and Latin churches and had helped to set the first Habsburg on the German throne, had been succeeded in twelve years by no less than seven popes, and now after a long interregnum and the unhappy experience of an eighth pope, Celestine, the Cardinal Caetani was to have his day. That he had encouraged Celestine to resign is more than likely. He can have felt no doubts on the wisdom of that step, just as he had no hesitation in quashing the hasty and ill-advised bulls issued during Celestine's pontificate. Everywhere about him, as he surveyed the political debris left by his predecessors, he saw work waiting to be done. Four years earlier the last Christian stronghold in Syria had fallen. The Holy Land, lying between the Sultanate of Egypt and the Mongolian conquerors of Persia and Mesopotamia, might yet be rescued if the still powerful schismatic churches in the East, the Jacobite and the Nestorian, could be strengthened in their task of converting the Mongols by the intervention of Rome. The affairs of Germany, of Hungary, of Poland demanded attention. Within the ecclesiastical system, many problems, such as the ever-present problem of the relations between the secular and regular clergy, called for decision. But above all, the Sicilian question—the legacy of the Holy War against the Emperor Frederick II and his family—must first be settled. We can see now that the question of Sicily was the beginning of modern political history. Frederick had succeeded the Normans as king of Sicily and South Italy. As emperor, he was unwilling to play the profitable Norman role of vassal and defender of the Holy See. In the course of a fierce crusade he had held his own, but after his death his family had been worn down and destroyed. The French prince, Charles of Anjou, had been called in, subvented partly by the proceeds of crusading taxes, partly by Florentine bankers; but before Charles died the island of Sicily had revolted and had called in the house of Aragon, which had in its service the greatest sailors of the age. So began the long struggle for the control of the Western Mediterranean. The outcome was the partition of Italy and the rivalries which alined the powers of Europe from the days of Ferdinand and Isabella to the days of Napoleon. But the popes of the later thirteenth century saw in the Sicilian question a rebellious island, the centre of an unrest threatening the peace of Europe and the stability of the Holy See in Italy. When Boniface VIII became pope he found a state of chaos, but he saw his way to a solution. Charles II of Sicily had failed to recover the coveted island, but the victorious house of Aragon, the political heirs of the Hohenstaufen, was divided against itself. On his succession to the throne of Aragon, King James II had hoped to combine the crowns of Aragon and Sicily. The independent islanders preferred his brother Frederick. James and Frederick did not see eye to eye in the matter. They were isolated. The one saw his Spanish Kingdom threatened by his old enemy, France; the other could no longer rely on the soldiers of Aragon and the ships of Genoa. The Pope, in a few months, effected what seemed likely to be a lasting settlement: peace between Aragon and France, a marriage treaty between the houses of Aragon and Anjou, ultimate compensation to James and Frederick alike for the loss of Sicily, the reunion of Sicily and Naples. It was his first great triumph. But it was short-lived. The Sicilians were obstinate and Frederick was crowned king. The Pope declared a new Holy War against the traitors. During nearly the whole of his reign this war wasted his resources and the resources of Europe. He had to pay for it. James of Aragon, Charles II of Anjou, and the Pope's hired champion, Charles of Valois, brother of the king of France, received subsidies which, it has been estimated, reached a total of 1,225,000 florins. To meet this vast sum, Italy, in papal tenths, provided 400,000 florins. France 173,000, and England no less than 450,000.[1] This was the background to the dispute about clerical taxation. If, Boniface argued, the clergy of France and England were burdened with the expense of this sacred cause, their canonical protection against the demands of kings must be safeguarded. If, the Kings argued, the clergy can export its wealth to aid the wars of the Pope, it may well be expected to aid us in our and their own wars. The subtle Sphinx had renewed an old riddle.

[1] F. Baethgen, 'Quellen und Untersuchungen zur Geschichte der päpstlichen Hof- und Finanzverwaltung unter Bonifaz VIII', in *Quellen und Forschungen aus italienischen Archiven und Bibliotheken* (1928–9), xx. 186, 187.

The Sicilian Crusade was, as I have said, the legacy of the struggle with Frederick II and the Hohenstaufen. The viper brood was by no means dead. The daughter of the great Manfred, Frederick's son, was, it is true, reconciled to the Church. She was the mother of James of Aragon and had given a son and daughter in marriage to children of the house of Anjou. But she was also the mother of Frederick of Sicily, and two of her brothers still lingered in the dungeons of Naples. Pope Boniface could not silence memory by a marriage contract. The Crusade stirred old passions among the Ghibellines of Italy. To what extent the terrible *vendetta* between Boniface and the family of the Colonna was due to its sympathy with Frederick of Sicily is uncertain; but the relations between the Colonna and the man whom Boniface regarded as a schismatic and a traitor certainly fed the anger of the Pope, and added to his difficulties. This powerful family turned against Boniface. The two cardinals of Colonna, who had voted for his election, took the lead in the local resistance to him, and, combining with Jacopone da Todi, the Franciscan poet, denied the validity of his election. They and their neighbours in the Campagna had other good grounds for resentment. Boniface from the first made it perfectly clear that he meant to be master in the Papal States and to rely for aid upon his family. He had amassed a fortune as cardinal and he used his private wealth and his prestige as pope to build up a great barony for his grand-nephew. The acquisitions of the Caetani, won by marriage and purchase, stretched from Anagni to the sea and for fifty miles along the coast, well into the kingdom of Naples. As time went on other great properties, confiscated from the heiress of the Aldobrandeschi, came to another grand-nephew in Tuscany. As the policy of Boniface became clear, the anti-papal party formed, members of the house of Colonna at its head. One of them, Stephen, a vigorous and cultivated layman, who lived to sound the praises of Petrarch and lives still in Petrarch's letters, seized the treasure of the Pope as it was being conveyed from Anagni to Rome. This exploit was hailed by the Joachimites and Spirituals as a proof of God's detestation of the luxury of the Church.

The treasure was returned, but by this time Boniface was implacable. All the weapons of the Holy War—the preaching of a crusade, excommunication, the inquisition—were turned against the Colonna. Their lands and castles were seized, their stronghold of Palestrina, full of precious relics of past ages, was razed to the ground. In the old Roman manner, the plough was passed over it, and salt sown on it. Stephen Colonna, the new Scipio, wandered in exile, Jacopone da Todi was imprisoned. The two cardinals, in spite of a submission, which Boniface received in conclave, wearing the tiara 'as a sign of the unity of the Church', were deprived. They passed, like Dante, from one refuge to another, and at last, like Stephen, made their way to France.

Boniface beat down these cardinals with the pitiless logic with which his predecessors had destroyed the Hohenstaufen, and a plausible defence of his action could doubtless be made; but a crusade against members of the Sacred College was so strange and monstrous that it raised in men's minds the issue of the moral responsibility of popes, not only to God, but to the Church. It was the heaviest count against a pope whom many regarded as a simoniac and were soon to regard as a heretic. Was it just that such a man should not be subject to the will of the Church? The possibility, admitted in theology, now threatened to become a very embarrassing fact. The moral issue is brought out clearly by Dante in his terrible verses on the tragedy of Palestrina. This prince of the new Pharisees was waging war not against Saracens or Jews, but in the neighbourhood of the Lateran. Every enemy of his was a Christian. Not one of them had helped to conquer Acre, the last Christian stronghold in Syria, not one of them had trafficked as a merchant in Egypt, a crime which at this time put a merchant outside the pale.

Dante drew a sharp distinction between the Pope and the man. Perhaps, so Professor Fedele has suggested, he heard the oration made by Boniface's successor at Perugia in June 1304, when the bull *Flagitiosum scelus* was issued against the persecutors of Boniface at Anagni.[1] Certainly,

[1] P. Fedele, 'Per la storia dell'attentato di Anagni', in *Bullettino dell'Istituto storico italiano* (1921), xli. 210–12.

his denunciation of the attack upon the Vicar of Christ, in whose person Christ suffered again the agonies of the Crucifixion, was inspired by that speech, which he turned into solemn music. But Boniface too easily confused the Pope with Benedict Caetani. It is true that he kept apart the papal from his personal treasure, using the latter for the aggrandizement of his family.[1] He was elected by cities of the Patrimony as their *podesta* under his family name. He arbitrated on one occasion between the kings of France and England—for so they insisted—not as pope but as Benedict. Yet this extraordinary man was incapable of self-scrutiny. As Mr. Previté-Orton has said, 'the most ecumenic and the narrowest aims met one another in his violent nature, without apparently a suspicion arising in his mind of their discrepancy, and it was this attempt to blend incompatibles which more than anything else caused his ruin'.[2] The publication of the archives of Aragon, which include the vivid and strictly contemporary dispatches of Aragonese envoys at the papal court, has helped to reveal him, to explain both the cause of the intense personal hatred which he could arouse and the element of truth in the extravagant charges brought against him by the Colonna and the agents of Philip of France. The type is not uncommon in history, but has only once been found upon the papal throne, varied though its occupants have been. Boniface had all the qualities of a very great pope save personal holiness and self-restraint. He was dignified and noble in appearance, decisive and vigorous, a master of business, a subtle canonist expert in explaining the meaning of terms and expounding the equitable rules of law. When he was not dominated by arrogance or passion, he could adjust himself to circumstance. 'The coarse-mouthed bully' could 'disappear for the moment in the skilful lawyer'.[3] His handling of the first controversy with Philip the Fair, opened in 1296 by the bull *Clericis laicos*, was reason-

[1] It seems, however, that there was some justification for the charge that Boniface also had recourse to the papal revenues for this purpose; see Boase, op. cit., pp. 160, 374.

[2] C. W. Previté-Orton, 'The Roman House of Caetani in the Middle Ages', in *Edinburgh Review* (Oct. 1928), p. 297.

[3] Boase, op. cit., p. 286.

able, his compromise between facts and principles skilful. The distinguished lawyers who, under his commission, added the Sext or sixth book to the Decretals turned to him in cases of difficulty as an expert. His registers reveal in all its complexity the range of papal business to which he succeeded. Other documents in the archives throw light on the collection of papal tenths and the relations with Italian bankers. The careful accounts of his household survive from two years, in little paper books bound in white parchment. The three banking firms employed by the Pope received the normal revenues from all sources, and took it in turns to settle the accounts of the household in the papal chamber. Boniface, determined to maintain his authority in the papal states, added a number of knights and men-at-arms to the great household of officials, chaplains, ushers and the rest. It has been calculated that 425 persons received food and livery from the kitchen and pantry, the cellar and marshalsea, in the papal court alone, and that the annual expenditure, normal and casual, ranged in the neighbourhood of 100,000 florins. The significance of this sum may perhaps be realized if I add that the wages of the papal washerwoman, who presumably did not do all the washing herself, were equivalent to one florin a month. In addition we have to add the clerks of the chancery, and the writers of the papal penitentiary and papal chamber.[1] Boniface bore the responsibility of the insistent daily business suggested by the detailed life of this great establishment. A medieval pope might be as ascetic as St. Bernard, as unworldly as St. Francis, but he could not extricate himself, by a quick decision, from the duties of his supreme office, the accumulation of centuries, and insist that the most widespread and intricate of all governments, the framework and stay of all the activities of the Church, should be carried on by private inspiration, without revenues. To complain that Boniface was not a Celestine would be as absurd as to complain that Cromwell was not a Fifth Monarchy man. The real *gravamen* against Boniface was indeed the opposite of this, that, adequate though he was to the traditional task entrusted to him, he was the victim of his own temperament. He was

[1] For all this see Baethgen, op. cit. pp. 114–237 *passim*.

like a man of the finest physical gifts but without that tiny cerebral instrument which enables him to keep his balance. The adjective most frequently used by contemporaries to describe him was *magnanimus*, and he has come down the ages as the *magnanimus peccator*. This is not the Latin for Bunyan's Great-Heart, but means rather a man built on big lines, great in spirit. He was, in the words of one fourteenth-century writer, 'the most vigorous signor (*vigoroso signore*) who ever sat in the See of Rome'. Petrarch described him as the wonder of kings and peoples, indeed of the world. He did everything either in the grand manner or with extravagant abandonment. He was so completely identified with the traditions of the papacy, that he felt at liberty to do as he liked. As a cardinal and legate he had rated the assembled doctors of Paris as though they were schoolboys. He once refused to confirm a metropolitan because he did not approve of his face, which may have been right; but he told him so, which was certainly wrong. He insulted ambassadors and mocked the physical peculiarities of his cardinals. This man, who celebrated Mass and said the offices with all the intensity of his being, even to tears, could fling the penitential ashes into the face of a Ghibelline archbishop. He had at his service the most learned and devoted apologists among the theologians and canonists of his age, but he had no friends. He was admired by many, feared by all, loved by none. He seems to have been untouched by the spiritual and intellectual influences in which most men find the meaning of their vocation in life. He took the vocation for granted. Cardinals, theologians, canonists were his instruments; he had quite enough to do with them in any case. In private he preferred the company of those who could amuse him, however worthless he might know them to be. By nature he was inclined to be sceptical and sardonic, and to laugh at the follies and credulity of those with whom he had to do. He was interested in experiments and novelties, and as so often happens to men of his type was attracted by necromancy. His angry petulance was partly the result of the painful disease which at one time threatened to kill him, until he got relief from the famous physician, Arnold of Villanova, and we cannot wonder at his pleasure in the society of this interesting man who, keenly concerned as he was with all forms of inquiry, yet stood aloof from the dialectic of the schools. The versatile physician was disliked by the cardinals as a dangerous influence. 'Would that Master Arnold had not come to court,' they complained. Arnold was both an ardent papalist and interested in dangerous movements, mixed up with Spirituals and Joachimites and Averroists; and Pope Boniface was quite unprejudiced. He did not attack Spirituals and others because they were worse than other people, but because they opposed him and seemed likely to be a public danger. Then they became everything that was vile. Again, Boniface was not anti-French. His whole policy in Italy depended on French support. As a cardinal he had been suspected as a friend of France and he had his well-wishers in the French royal family; but when the French king and his advisers resisted his authority he was merciless. After the Jubilee of 1300, he put no restraint upon himself. The ambassador of Aragon wrote in 1301, 'Everyone wishes he was dead and deplores the outrageous things he says and does'. And the Englishman to whom we owe the best account of the attack on Anagni two years later tells how the whole country-side was roused against the Pope in his days of humiliation.

Rumour, inspired by hatred, quickly plays havoc with the reputation of such a man. The incredible *dossier* collected by his enemies after his death need not surprise us. The terms of the inquiry presented to the witnesses were drafted with great care, in the hope of avoiding all misunderstanding, but the witnesses were too carefully chosen and too sure of their ground to be embarrassed. Boniface had given them many openings, and the most harmless jibe could be used—probably quite conscientiously—as evidence of heresy. One day, for example, the admiral Roger Loria had rather unctuously enlarged upon the joys awaiting him in Paradise. The pope caustically replied, 'Maybe, maybe not'. This was used to prove that Boniface did not believe in a future life. A recalcitrant French bishop was ordered to erect a statue of a pope, so that he might not again forget his duty to the Head of the Church. This was used to suggest that Boniface was an idolater. Again Boniface was charged with incredulity; and it is quite possible that he had attended learned discussions on the merits of the three religions, Christianity, Mohammedanism, and Judaism. But such discussions were common enough. Several works of that ardent missionary, Ramon Lull, are in the form of dialogues of this kind. We need not pay much heed to these charges, still less to the grosser accusations brought against Boniface. The truth is that he had a rough and caustic tongue, a brutal sense of humour, and an ungovernable temper, and that behind the lofty ecclesiasticism in which he so passionately believed, and of which he was such a dignified and vigorous exponent, there lurked the mundane passions, the curiosity, the love of fame, the self-confidence of a cultivated Italian nobleman. 'He who is healthy, rich and fortunate,' he is reported to have said, 'has Paradise on earth.' And one day he said to his physician, 'We have increased the Roman Church in so much gold and silver, that our memory will be glorious for evermore'.

Equal to every occasion, unhampered by self-questioning, Boniface moved on from his wars and vendettas, his dispute with France and his efforts to control the destiny of faction-ridden Florence, to the great year of the Jubilee. In this year 1300 he was, to all seeming, firm as a rock, as secure as any successor of St. Peter. Thousands of pilgrims passed daily from the shrine of St. Peter to the shrine of St. Paul. A plenary indulgence—hitherto granted only to crusaders—was open to all save the schismatics, Frederick of Sicily and the Colonna and the merchants who traded with the infidel. Christendom seemed to be united in Rome under the vicar of God. Boniface passed on to other triumphs. Towards the end of 1302 he put an end to the wasteful war with Sicily.[1] Frederick was to hold the throne for life, but the island was afterwards to revert to the house of Anjou. The Pope could well afford the compromise, for he had his eyes on a greater vassal. In a consistory of 30 April 1303

[1] The treaty of Caltabellotta, afterwards confirmed, with some modifications, by Boniface, was originally made by Charles of Valois without reference to the Pope, who was reluctant to grant peace. See Boase, op. cit., pp. 291–2, 332.

he received the ambassadors of Albert of Austria, king of Germany and emperor elect. They brought royal letters confirming an oath of fealty, more far-reaching than any oath of any German king to a pope, before or since—an oath modelled on that given by the officers who governed the Papal States. Boniface, in an oration, recognized Albert as king and set out in all its fullness the theory of the translation of the Empire, as it had been expounded by Pope Innocent IV. It was for the Pope to decide which favoured people should be the seat of empire. Albert's chancellor followed with a scholastic harangue in which he exalted the papal power and submitted to the papal doctrine. Then he and his colleagues took the oath on behalf of their master.

Within four months the servants of Philip of France and the fiercest of the Colonna had broken into the palace of Anagni. Within five months Boniface was dead. For ten years the Church was perplexed by the issue whether he was or was not a heretic and a criminal, subject, even in death, to the verdict of a council. Albert of Austria, quite unaffected, went on his astute way. He had got what he wanted, security of tenure. Rome resumed its life of family feuds and Italy its endless wars. And the popes, gradually realizing that their work could best be done elsewhere, settled down in Avignon.

When Boniface in the spring of 1303 came to an understanding with Albert of Austria he had for more than a year been involved in a hot dispute with Philip of France. The immediate cause was the proceedings of Philip against the bishop of Pamiers, a friend of the Pope: this raised the issue of the immunity of the clergy, an issue which was soon developed to cover the whole question of the relations between the secular and ecclesiastical powers. The Pope was determined to fight to a finish—a wild ambition, for this issue has never been fought to a finish without the disintegration of Europe. His elaborate argumentation in the bull *Ausculta fili* (5 Dec. 1301) was treated with contempt—the rumour spread that it had been thrown on the fire. A misleading and abbreviated version—a medieval Ems telegram—was circulated. Its blunt phrasing—'It is our will that you be subject to us in temporal and spiritual things'—rallied the nobility of France, for St. Louis himself, whom Boniface had recently canonized, would have repudiated such doctrine. The clergy were disunited and hesitant. The States-General, meeting in Notre-Dame, supported the King. The Pope stood firm. He was encouraged by the disastrous defeat of the French army in Flanders in July 1302, he counted upon the support of Albert of Austria, Philip's former ally. Soon after a council held on All Saints' Day to which he had summoned the leading French clergy, he issued the bull *Unam Sanctam*. Philip temporized, whether from genuine hesitation or policy is still disputed. He offered to discuss the issues in dispute. The Pope, through his legate, demanded a definite answer and reminded him that, by putting obstacles in the way of free intercourse between Rome and France, he was already excommunicate. The King, in June 1303, appealed to a council of the Church. Throughout France his emissaries secured the adhesion of local governments and towns. He could rely on the nobles and most of the secular clergy, and even the Franciscans were equally divided between king and pope.

The national rally against Pope Boniface was largely due to a man who, after some years in the royal service, had lately won the ear of the King. This was William of Nogaret, a native of the county of Toulouse, and a former professor of law in Montpellier. There is no good ground to reject the story that William's father and mother had been burned as heretics. He came from a land full of bitter memories. He belonged to a people whose sceptical, but passionate, outlook had no room for the tenacious orthodoxy and disciplined traditions which made compromise in its relations with the Church almost a matter of principle at the French court. Nogaret was a clerk in minor orders, *magister* as well as *miles regis*; he could quote Scripture and St. Augustine with the facility of a schoolman; he professed at every turn to be serving the true interests of the Church; and he had a very definite idea of the part which the king of France, the eldest son of the Church, should play. He was more obstinate than Boniface himself, and he was carried along by a cold fury more sinister and dreadful than Boniface's hot passion. Before the papal ultimatum was written, Philip and he were prepared. On 7 March 1303 he, with three others, received full powers to act in the royal interests. On 12 March, in council, he outlined his policy. Boniface was a false prophet, a heretic and man of evil life, who had not entered the sheepfold by the door, but had climbed in by another way. In the interests of the Church, and to avoid schism, the Pope must be secured and a faithful shepherd of the sheep appointed. The king of France, following in the footsteps of his ancestors, must come to the aid of our mother, the Roman Church, and strike her fetters from her. King Philip, who had more discreet counsellors about him, moved more cautiously. He preferred to arouse public opinion, to invite the support of the princes of Christendom, and to appeal to a council; but when Nogaret had arrived in Italy with his companions in August, he followed his own plan, with or without instructions from his master. The Florentine bankers of Philip provided the money, the enemies of Boniface joined his small force. The Pope had prepared a bull of deposition, freeing Philip's subjects from their duty to the King, and Nogaret decided to anticipate its publication. At Ferentino in the Campagna, a few miles from Anagni, where Boniface was passing the summer, he made his plans with Sciarra Colonna, Rinaldo da Supino, who had suffered more humiliation than most at the hands of Boniface, and many other barons. They had friends in Anagni and accomplices in the papal court itself. Nogaret and his force, 600 horse and 1,000 foot, entered the city at dawn on 7 September, by a northern gate on the height near the fortified Castello, where the papal palace, the Caetani quarter, and the houses of the cardinals, with their alleys and gardens, lay along the piazza of the cathedral. In the dim light they clattered up the narrow street to the Castello, with the standard of the Church and the banner of France waving above them. Men and women, roused by their cries, leapt from their beds and rushed to their doors. Later in the day, after fruitless parleys, the conspirators forced their way through the cathedral and back through the houses and gardens till they had reached the papal palace. The resistance of the Caetani was fierce but short. In a tumultuous assembly the bewildered citizens elected Adenolfo di Papa, one of the enemies of Boniface, captain of the people.

When the conspirators at last broke into the presence of Boniface, Nogaret was busy elsewhere. It was Sciarra Colonna who insulted and perhaps struck the Pope, as he sat, deserted by all but two cardinals, in his papal chair, the papal crown on his head, the cross in his hands. Then Nogaret came and told him that he was to be brought to judgement before a council of the Church. But the scandal was too great. Within three days a counter-revolution had cleared the city, and Boniface was brought to Rome. He was a sick and broken-hearted man. He had escaped the Colonna to fall into the more friendly care of the Orsini. Help might have come from Naples and from Frederick of Sicily, with whom he had been so wisely reconciled; but his day was over. On 11 October he died quietly, after making his confession in the presence of eight cardinals.

Dramatic symbolism, which coloured the mind of men in those days, gave the life of Boniface a setting of thunder and darkness. When in 1291 he said his first Mass at Orvieto, and more candles were lit in the church because of the darkness of the day, men saw an augury of schism and war. A thunderstorm appropriately cut short the ceremony of his burial. Stories of his last days, of his madness and despair and blasphemies, were spread abroad. For ten years a dismal warfare was waged against his memory, while he lay in the splendid tomb which Arnolfo di Cambio at his command had prepared for him in the church of St. Peter. But now, in Renan's fine phrase, he has entered into the serenity of history; and we can see him more clearly, a man who, if he had not been the victim of his own impulses, might have been planned by nature to be the master of the world.

Boniface, unhappily for himself, lived in a time which needed a pope as great as himself but wiser, more temperate, more far-seeing. It was a time when the rich experience of the past was in flower, when poets and artists, mystics, theologians and canonists, princes and statesmen, travellers and merchants, were becoming conscious of their inheritance, when the creative and reflective powers were free and new horizons were opening. We should not set one activity against another as more far-reaching or more enlightened, for all alike were rooted in the past, and opened out under the same sky. While Boniface was pope, Duns Scotus, his mind stored with the vigorous dialectic of a century, was lecturing on the Sentences at Oxford and Paris. At Paris, too, in the Dominican convent, Master Eckhart was learning to sound, as he alone has ever been able to sound, the depths of the soul. Giotto was at work on his frescoes in the churches of Rome, Villani on the history of Florence which the sight of Rome during the Jubilee had inspired. Marco Polo was dictating at Genoa his description of the Mongol Empire in China. It was the age of Dante, of Olivi, of Ramon Lull, Arnold of Villanova, of the great Italian Spirituals. At no time in history have more fine spirits been alive to the riches of the visible and the invisible. And at no time were men more aware of the dangers which beset the unity of the Christian world, as the wealth of experience, the rights of states, the infinite possibilities of commerce and money and social life were revealed. In the long discipline of centuries all this richness had been stored, and now the unity which it had been the object of the Church to conserve and enrich was threatened by the Church's own children. Boniface was not the man to guide Europe into the way of peace, or to unite Christendom in a Holy War, but, in his efforts to do so, he was sustained by forces far greater and purer than his own imperious will. He had behind him the traditions of the medieval Church.

IV

MEDIEVAL EDUCATION[1]

WHEN in these days people meet to talk about education, they take some very important things for granted. They assume that there is such a thing as a national system of education; and they assume that knowledge, the main element in education, should be sought for its own sake. Sooner or later they find that it is not easy to reconcile the two things, although each seems so obvious and beyond dispute. Those people who lay most stress on the importance of a national system of education begin to wonder whether, after all, knowledge should be sought for its own sake; they argue that it should be regarded as subordinate to a wider ideal of education, though they differ very much when they try to define an ideal system of national education. In the same way, those people who lay most stress on knowledge begin to wonder whether, after all, it is right to regard education from a national point of view. They point out that knowledge means mental freedom, although many young people do not seem to be mentally so constructed as to be able to acquire it. Moreover, the fact that men and women happen to be collected in cities and states has nothing to do with the pursuit of truth for its own sake. Then wise persons try to bring the parties together again. They explain that the parties are not really at variance. A national system of education, they point out, has in mind the range within which the system works, not so much the kind or content of education. Everybody in a state ought to be educated if he is to take his place in social life, but we educate him by trying to make him intelligently aware of his surroundings and able to express himself. We must be careful, they go on, not to try to turn out people all of one pattern nor to think only of the particular things they are going to do. In progressive society vocational training except as part of something bigger is impossible, for it implies a sort of

[1] A lecture given to the City of London Vacation Course, 2 August 1932.

caste system, and these are the days of equal opportunity for all. At the same time, while we teach things for their own sake, because it is a good thing in itself to be able to use one's mind, we must not forget that learning is a dangerous thing, and that a little learning is a very dangerous thing; we must not neglect moral and physical health, nor, if we can agree, spiritual health. For a little while these wise people may make peace, but only for a little while. Their wisdom sounds well, but somehow or other it does not seem to help very much. The crowd of children who forget all they ever learned as quickly as possible, and misuse their ability to read and write, is as large as ever. The quarrel begins all over again. Nobody wants to go back to the days before 1870, yet nobody is happy about our education. Something is wrong somewhere, and we probably end with the reflection that there must be waste and frustration in any system, and that on the whole we are improving.

If we could have here one of the great medieval thinkers, what would he say about it all? I fancy that he would say something like this: 'I do not know what you mean when you talk about education in the way that I hear you talk. You speak of education for a nation, of education with a big E. But what is a nation? It is a natural division or group of men under a ruler or government. It is divided into districts and cities, and homes which also are natural groups of men. Each of these groups, from the home upwards, has an end, as the philosopher, Aristotle, teaches, but these are not ends in themselves. I can understand you if you say that the father ought to be taught how to manage his family, or the magistrate his city, or the official his district, or the ruler his kingdom. We had a great many books about these things, especially about the duties of rulers. But I do not understand your idea of educating everybody in the same way, or in two or three ways—boys and girls, young men and women of all kinds, whatever they are going to be or do. I know that by nature all men are equal and that they are equal in the eyes of God, but since the Fall of man they have had to labour each in the place allotted to him. As the Apostle says, there is the same spirit, but a diversity of gifts. The people who work with their hands in the fields or at a craft maintain the state of the world. The knightly class protect it. The clergy prepare it for the life to come, which is the great end which all other ends serve; and you yourselves seem to admit that these should be taught differently, though I see all kinds of people at the universities besides the clergy and lawyers and doctors. I am puzzled by your elementary and secondary schools. Surely there is great danger in teaching all kinds of people so many things which they cannot grasp and which will not be of use to them. Nor do I understand you when you talk about progress, for you seem to mix up growing in justice and peace and ability to live a life of reason and intellectual pleasure with so many other things, and you seem to have the most curious ideas about what the end of it all is. You seem to leave God out. Perhaps this is in part because you talk so much of knowledge for its own sake. I think that you should distinguish more clearly, as we did, between the practical and the contemplative life. Everybody ought to be trained in the practical work which he has to do, though he need not go to school to be trained. And, if the rulers do their work properly, and people listen to those who preach to them, and are obedient to their rulers and to God, there will be justice and peace in a land, so that everybody can take pleasure in life, so far as is possible in this world. We used to rejoice when rulers took an interest in knowledge. But the pursuit of knowledge as such is a very difficult thing. It is part of a life of contemplation; just as monks have their special kind of contemplation, so the scholar must put himself under some discipline, and, in his pursuit of knowledge, try to avoid pride and vanity of words, and to remember that his first duty, like everybody's, and, perhaps especially in his case, his most responsible duty, is to God. You seem to me to separate learning from duty and contemplation too much, although I rather like the ideals of a scholar which I have read in your books. One of our teachers, Hugh of St. Victor, said that, in proceeding from the known to the unknown, the scholar should keep a humble mind, an earnest desire for investigation, a quiet life, a silent brooding survey, and that he should be poor and live in a strange land. All the same, I admire your interest in education, and I rejoice in many of your ideas. It is a pity that you are so restless. Your new schools and old university buildings and libraries are wonderful. Paris was very noisy and uncomfortable when I studied there.'

If we look a little more closely into the mind of our imaginary scholar, we may be impressed by two of his phrases: 'everybody should be trained in the work which he has to do' and that phrase from Hugh of St. Victor, the scholar 'should be poor and live in a strange land'. In the medieval world we do not find any departments of education; we hear little or nothing about an educational ladder or equality of opportunity. What we call education as a separate activity of the community was then part of the moral life, part of the discipline which was needed to keep any person and order, every trade or profession, healthy. As we shall see later, the idea of public support, and even public provision of educational activity was by no means unfamiliar. We find village schools and town schools, and teachers paid by the community. In higher education we find valuable endowments. We find numerous instances of men who became great and famous, or very useful to society, because they had availed themselves of what we term educational opportunity. We find idealists who anticipated, here and there, some of our modern ideas and developments. Yet, in the nature of the case, the idealism which in the Middle Ages corresponded to our educational idealism was nothing more nor less than the desire that every man should live the good life and do honestly what God had given him to do. The medieval tracts about education—and they are very numerous—are moral tracts. They deal with behaviour and cover a wide ground. They were written for particular kinds of people, or as guides to those in authority, to show how they were to direct the persons committed to their charge. They are practical. I do not think that any difference in intention separates the handbooks for rulers from the guides for the country clergy or the books about the art of professional writing for scribes and notaries or the treatises on hawking or the care of horses. Everybody required technical instruction, whether he was going to preach or to sail a boat. Some technical instruction, of course, involved more moral training than others, but on the other hand all technical instruction was given within the surroundings in which one lived and was generally acquired from one's family or employer or guild. As a rule, a boy did not go out to be educated and then come back to work. Hence, however technical his work might be, he was not separated from the traditional social life, or if he were, he became part of another. Our modern educational systems were forced upon us because—at least this was one reason—without them, we could not cope with the problems of industrialism and the intellectual demands of modern science. These had broken into the texture of our social life and threatened to destroy it. Social activities were no longer subsidiary to the old framework of home, village community, town organization, and national government. The old framework rather, was—as it increasingly is—being swallowed up, or twisted, or, at the best, reshaped by our new social activities. In the Middle Ages this was not the case. The texture was there, changing and becoming more intricate, but unbroken, except by war and plague which made it seem all the more precious and inevitable. In the eyes of wise men it was alive in every part, alive with moral opportunity. It was the task of the good to see that its life was preserved, that the useless and rebellious threads, so to speak, did not tangle it.

We must not suppose that the texture of medieval society was dull and drab. It was full of life and colour; indeed, the constant preoccupation of the medieval ruler with order and discipline was due to the difficulty of keeping it unbroken and clean. A medieval ruler was rather like Penelope, with the difference that as a rule he did not undo his work himself but was surrounded by people only too willing to undo it for him. When life is eager and vigorous, education is the regulation not the awakening of life; it opens windows, but has no need to drag people to look out of them. A great German preacher, Berthold of Regensburg, who lived in the thirteenth century, was once preaching to the people on the seven planets. He said: 'Although you lay folk cannot read as we priests can, yet God has given you two books to read . . . one is the heavens, the other the earth.' It was the preacher's task to show the way to people who, in every walk of life, were born into a world of custom mingled with excitement, a world with established traditions, yet passionate and violent, where sorrow and merriment alike were stark realities, and the spirit of adventure was, when aroused, incalculable, impelling, fierce with a consuming desire for action and knowledge, for the cup of evil or for surrender to the good. One of the seven deadly sins was what we call boredom, what theologians and moralists called *accidia*—just the kind of mood which would overcome a disillusioned monk, when the high spirit of adventure had passed, but a sin, wherever found, in medieval eyes. In his *Inferno* Dante placed people of this kind in the slime of the marsh called Styx—they sob under the water and make it bubble on the surface. 'We were sullen in the sweet air which is made glad by the sun: we carried lazy smoke within our hearts.' And on the outskirts of Hell, spurned by Hell no less than by Heaven, in the starless air, Dante put those who were neither good nor bad, but had dragged on drearily and timidly, without praise and without blame. They have no hope of death, for they never were alive, and they run incessantly, goaded by wasps and hornets. In the days of Dante men were often the victims of a hot or cold fury against the powers that be, of wilful or calculated rebellion, even of despair; but they were not paralysed as we so easily are, by the thought of slow, remorseless, and impersonal evolution. The world was God's creation, a place of discipline, and man must seize his opportunity. He did not acquiesce in what Shakespeare calls 'the thievish progress to eternity'.

This is the spirit in which Hugh of St. Victor said that the scholar should live in poverty in an alien land. St. Hugh was a monk, and there is more than an echo of the monastic idea in his words. Here we are in a foreign land, and if we would be ready for our real home, we must free ourselves from the pride and vanities of this temporary world. But the call to adventure is there also. In St. Hugh's time—he lived in the twelfth century, when Abelard and St. Bernard lived—in his time and for long after, the search for knowledge was an adventure, just as the monastic life and the Crusades and the creations of art and poetry were full of the spirit of adventure. This was the age of the great cathedral schools, one of which was to grow into the University of Paris, of the appropriation of the Roman law and the systematizing of canon law and theology, of the diffusion of Greek and Arabic science. In the course of the next century, the *Studium* came to be regarded as one of the three functions of organized social life, side by side with the *Imperium*, or political, and the *Sacerdotium*, or priestly ecclesiastical function. Moreover, like men in other ways of life, the scholar was, more often than not, a young man. The Middle Ages were a time of youth rather than of age, and young men frequently exhausted themselves in their feverish eagerness. They were old at forty. St. Bernard was a youth of about twenty when he and his companions appeared before the gate of Citeaux and asked leave to enter the monastery. St. Thomas Aquinas did most of his great work before he was forty and was only forty-seven when he died. Two of the most arduous achievements of medieval scholarship in the study of law, the gloss of Accursius on the Code of Justinian, and the work of Bartolus, who laid the foundations of our private international law, were done by young Italians before the age of forty: Accursius lived to be an old man, but his work was done in youth, Bartolus died at the age of forty-three. Now it would certainly be a mistake to suppose that all these great men or most of the crowds who flocked to the medieval university lived lives of poverty in an alien land. Many studied in their native country, most adopted professional careers in church and state. But nearly all had to struggle, to live on very little far from home, and, if they were to succeed, had to devote all their strength of mind and body to the pursuit of knowledge during many years. Hence, when we think of medieval education, we must distinguish the life of the Universities from the normal everyday training in home and school, in the shop and on the ship, or even in the cathedral and the monastery which had preceded the universities as homes of learning. In course of time the universities tended to become more local in their character, less intense in their activity; but right through and, indeed, until the end of the seventeenth century, we find the spirit of adventure, the scholars who wander in search of new learning, and spend all their lives in poverty and discomfort. One thinks of Erasmus, of Clenardus, who at the end of the sixteenth century went to Portugal and Africa in search of Arabic teachers, of Descartes, with his almost monastic ideals of seclusion, of the Prussian David Wilke, who after wandering from one European university to another, found a comfortable home in England, and, under his English name, Wilkins, is regarded as one of our great scholars. In these and other equally famous men of the sixteenth and seventeenth centuries we see the temper of the medieval scholar.

May I add, at this point, that we should distinguish the wandering scholars of this type, men to whom travel was a means to an end, from the wandering scholars, the vagrants or goliards, whom Miss Helen Waddell and other writers have lately brought to life again? These fascinating vagabonds made travel a profession. They were the gipsies of the learned world, or, at their worst, the parasitic element in the academic life. They were part of the floating population of medieval Europe, like the professional singers or *jongleurs*, or the more harmful mercenaries and 'free companies'. Like every other body of men, they had their customs and strange codes—even their text-books, immoral parodies of other text-books, on the art of love and the like. Their poets composed delightful songs about the hard life of the scholar and the joys of women and wine.[1] But they were not the real thing, and they did not last very long. The real thing was more prosaic—a boy or young man bitten by the desire to learn, hard put to it for money, or supported from the revenue of his church by a bursary or prebend, in the hope that he would come back to be a credit and a strength to it. Ecclesiastical legislation encouraged him, while it attacked the goliard.

[1] It should be noted, however, that much 'goliardic' poetry was not written by goliards at all.

These general observations will, I hope, have made clear the importance of distinguishing, in the first place, between university education, where elementary instruction of boys was regarded as preliminary to a long and arduous course of study, and such organized instruction as existed outside the universities. I hope it is also clear that what I may call unregulated, social, almost instinctive education was, in the nature of things, more widespread and significant, if compared with systematic education, than it is to-day. It is very hard indeed to give any idea of the measure and value of this unregulated natural instruction, for it was so intangible as well as so real. For example, people will always differ, I imagine, about the value and range of moral and mental discipline in the medieval village. A strong case can be made out for Dr. Coulton's statement: 'That jealousy of primary education, which remains one of the vividest political pictures in the minds of those who remember the struggle of 1870 and the following years, must be multiplied fourfold when we think ourselves back to the Middle Ages.'[1] The statement is a little misleading, because it suggests theories of the state and of society which, as I have tried to show, did not exist; one can hardly be jealous of the inconceivable. Moreover, the Church had very clear ideas about the kind of guidance which the peasantry should get. It was the duty of every parish priest to instruct his flock and, in particular, to see that the children were taught the Lord's Prayer, and the Creed. In some dioceses, as in St. Omer in 1183, the building of schools near every parish church and the appointment of paid teachers were enjoined, and, although general provision of this kind cannot be found, village schools were by no means uncommon in the Middle Ages; they can be traced in several parts of France, for example, in the thirteenth and fourteenth centuries. But the real issue does not lie here: it lies in the problem, how far was the village community affected by the influence and guidance of its clergy, by a moral and religious atmosphere which could purify traditional paganism, by all the singing and mural pictures and festivals of the church, by inducements to good workmanship, and restraint

[1] G. G. Coulton, *The Medieval Village*, p. 254.

and peace in social life? On all these matters there is, as one would expect, a bewildering variety of evidence. It is absurd to suppose that, taken as a whole, the parish clergy were a well-educated and spiritual class of men, or that social life was pure, or work in field and barn done eagerly in a spirit of good fellowship. It is equally absurd to talk as though the stock from which the people of modern Europe have sprung was not essentially healthy in mind and body. While there were few, if any, distractions from outside, the opportunities for a rounded and good life were more incessant then than now; and though only a man or woman here and there took full advantage of them, the common life was fuller, better, and more generous because of them. The medieval preachers knew all about it. As a twelfth-century homilist said: 'Many throughout all the earth have eagerly received faith in the Saviour and his teaching, and so they shall do continually until the end of the world.' We must leave the matter there. Our country-folk were *alive*, and where there is life, there is hope. The best educational system is a poor, anaemic, struggling thing, if it has not got living, alert minds and bodies to work upon.

When we leave the village-folk and turn to the more mobile elements in medieval society, we seem to be in a different world. Quite apart from systematic education as we regard it, there was no lack of instruction there. Indeed, it would be easy to write a description of medieval society in which almost everybody would seem to be teaching everybody else—as, of course, in one sense everybody was. I have spoken of the large number of books written about the education of kings and princes; the last thing which the medieval ruler suffered from was lack of good advice. Even popes were not exempt: one of the most outspoken books ever written is St. Bernard's little treatise, *De consideratione*, addressed to his friend, Pope Eugenius III. It was all very good, practical advice, and intensely edifying; perhaps it was too edifying. Medieval energy spent itself in exhortation and discussion just as it spent itself in fighting and going to law. These were the ways in which states and codes of law and behaviour were painfully developed.

The elaborate penitential system, the rules about confession, the free-spoken preaching, the disputations in the classroom, all of them were forms of discipline, of education. The training of novices in monasteries, when it fell into good hands, was a fine spiritual art. One of the most beautiful and living books I know is the book which Ailred, a young abbot of Rievaulx in Yorkshire, wrote about the training of novices. It was still used in the seventeenth century, and may perhaps be used still by those who know it. This same Ailred wrote another book about the way in which women who lived as recluses should behave; and a well-known passage is a good example of the universal love of instructing others. These holy women, says Ailred, should not run the risk of keeping informal schools for boys and girls, as some of them do. He gives a picture of a recluse, shut up in her cell by the church door. She sits at her window, the pupils sit in the porch. The good woman laughs at or with her young friends, blames them, draws them near and slaps them, flatters and kisses and embraces them—in short makes a shocking exhibition of herself. She ought not to do it.

About a hundred and fifty years later, that is about 1300, we find a very interesting concern with education. The Crusades had failed, and in various quarters, notably among the Franciscans and Dominicans, more emphasis was laid upon the value of missions as a means of converting the non-Christian peoples of the earth. One remarkable, if eccentric man, Ramon Lull, a Catalan from the Balearic Islands, spent his life in the effort to organize action on these lines. He helped to found a missionary college at Miramar in Majorca, for the study of Arabic and the training of missionary friars (1276). The college did very little, but lingered on in one form or another as a house of desultory 'Lullian science', until the nineteenth century. 'Lullian science' comprised, in Ramon's mind, ambitious systems of education. He was interested in training all kinds of people, not only missionaries. One of his innumerable books is a symbolic little treatise called *The Book of the Order of Chivalry*. Another is a didactic encyclopaedia which he called *The Doctrine for Boys*. Dealing with every manner of thing, it concentrates on the training of children, their beliefs, morals, food, clothes, and so on. Indeed, its teaching is not unlike some of the doctrines disseminated by our modern, more esoteric educationalists. A younger contemporary of Lull, a Norman lawyer, also wrote about educational ideals, as part of a plan for ‘the recovery of the Holy Land’. His book with this title was dedicated to the crusader, King Edward I of England. He drew his inspiration from history, a study whose value he was one of the first to emphasize. Just as in the ancient world successful war trod in the wake of learning, so it would be now, if Christian Europe would organize learning. And so Dubois wished to see a graduated system of schools—with a militant conversion of the heathen as the end to be kept in mind. He believed in the teaching of modern languages, on a more widespread scale than the friars had planned. It is useless, he says, to rely on interpreters. The best teachers of Eastern tongues must be procured. But this is only the culmination of a system which would begin with schools for children from four to six years of age. The children should be taken from home, and settled in groups of a hundred or so in fitting places. He believes that the kind of place chosen is important and that some tasks are more suitable than others for certain periods of the year. This stage of education should end at the age of twelve. Then come logic and languages, and then specialization in preaching, law, medicine, for the future missionaries. Medical care is a fruitful means of conversion. Dubois, indeed, thinks that instructed women, with some knowledge of medicine as well as of the Christian faith, ought to be sent out. They could become the wives of the marriageable Eastern clergy, and of intelligent infidels and schismatics, and heal them in body and soul.

Lull was a visionary, Dubois a doctrinaire, but they show how medieval society in the age of Dante was concerned with *training*. What happened, I think, was a more conscious realization of a fact, of which it was felt that more constructive use could be made—the fact that the various orders, groups, interests, and crafts which made up the social body were maintained by growing traditions, passed on from one generation to another by deliberate instruction. The idea of a gentleman, which formed a code of chivalry, the responsible duties of a ruler or magistrate, the mysteries of a craft had to be taught; and they were taught, not in special schools—such as the clergy possessed—but in the households and guilds which kept the traditions alive. Take, for example, the masons' lodges at Strasbourg, one of the chief centres of the art of building from about the time of which I have been speaking, the time of Dante. There the builders, from the master to the young scholar or apprentice, belonged to a society. This society had its own life, customs, jurisdiction, punishments, means of training. Education within it was at once technical, moral, and religious. The boys, taken about the age of thirteen, were trained by the associates, and after a time—about five years—were submitted to examination in the history and technicalities of the stone-worker's craft. Only then could the novice use his own mark and go on his travels as a trained mason. The training of the builder was merely a more systematic example of the domestic education which every aspect of medieval life involved.

From such a soil schools would naturally rise, for it is obvious that, especially in the towns, a great deal of unnecessary labour could be avoided in the more efficient activity of the schoolroom. The Church had taken the lead in the foundation of schools, and during the four centuries which followed the time of Charles the Great—the last ruler who had a definite educational policy of his own—the Church had charge of all the systematic education which existed. Hence, when in the later Middle Ages, that is to say, from about the year 1200 onwards, municipal or communal schools gradually made headway, and lay teachers, especially in Italy, became common, the methods and content of teaching had already been defined by the long experience of monastic and diocesan schools, primarily or entirely intended for the instruction of clerks. Although it is clear that the laity benefited from these schools—again more especially in the diocesan schools of Italy—it was unusual for the aristocracy to send their children to them, unless they were intended for an ecclesiastical career, while, at the other end of the social scale, the sons of peasants would rarely be found in them, and then only if they had been picked out for training as clerks. In other words the ecclesiastical schools were intended for the future clergy, but were, to a greater or less degree, open to the sons of gentry and merchants, who were not destined for ecclesiastical life. As time passed, other schools were founded, always influenced by the traditions of the ecclesiastical schools, but of a more secular character. These were as a rule maintained by the city or town authorities and, at all events in Italy, were often controlled by lay teachers.

Any general description of the ecclesiastical schools must suffer from the fact that we are dealing with a variety of conditions in very different countries or communities throughout a long period. In the later Middle Ages, for example, the monasteries can be almost entirely neglected as centres of education except for their own oblates and novices. Ecclesiastical reformers did not like to see groups of boys and girls associated with monasteries and nunneries, just as Ailred did not like to see anchoresses consorting with the young girls of the neighbourhood. The few cases of grammar schools attached to monasteries have been shown to be exceptional or to have been derived from lay foundations. The impressive educational system of the Dominicans was, of course, intended for the Dominicans themselves. Even in earlier times, when monastic schools, open to outsiders, were more common, they were less important than the diocesan schools, controlled by the cathedral and greater churches, and the system under which the educational life of the diocese was under the control of a high official, the magiscola, or archdeacon or chancellor. Here, again, the significance of the church schools lies, not so much in the fact that, in a greater or less degree, they admitted the laity—for they were primarily and in the main schools for clerks—but in the fact that the system provided a sort of framework, into which schools of a different type could gradually be fitted. The licence to teach was, for a long time, a licence given by an ecclesiastic, the archdeacon or the chancellor. The masters of most schools, whether church or endowed grammar schools or communal schools, were—except in the Italian cities—clerks. The development of education involved at every step co-operation with the Church, and in general, though not always, submission to the rules and practices gradually devised under the direction of popes, councils, and bishops. Similarly, the traditions of teaching were derived from ecclesiastical education and only gradually became free. The process was much more gradual, the tradition much more tenacious, than would appear from an isolated study of the great humanist educationalists, such as Guarino and Vittorino, of fifteenth- and sixteenth-century Italy. Just as the so-called humanism has its roots deep in the past, so the medieval methods survived in Protestant countries in the seventeenth century. When considered from a broad standpoint, the history of education is but one aspect of the slow uneasy history of European society.

The foundation in all schools was grammar. In an ordinary church school the boys from about seven to nine or ten, in the lower or *minor* school, learned to read and write and speak Latin with the aid of the Psalter, to sing, and to reckon or count. They would learn the Creed and the works of mercy and about the cardinal virtues and vices. Then in the higher school would come more thorough grounding in grammar and syntax, studied in well-known text-books, and simple Latin literature, both religious and profane, with explanations of the history and mythology and geography—all leading up to the more advanced study comprised under the head of Dialectic. The method of teaching was repetition, and in the more advanced courses, discussion. Here is a fragment of dialogue from a little book used a good deal in German schools, *Es tu scholaris?* 'Why are you a scholar?' the little student is asked. 'Because I go to school and learn letters' (the word *litterae* has a general sense). 'What do you do?' 'I get up in the morning, dress at once, brush my hair, wash my hands, pray to God, and go to school gladly.' 'What do you read?' 'I do not read, I listen.' 'What do you hear?' 'Donatus or Alexander or logic or music.' Then he explains why it is necessary to avoid the company of women and laymen, for this is a school for young clerks. Now, when we come to the municipal schools, started in Germany in the thirteenth and fourteenth centuries, we find a very similar sort of instruction. They are grammar schools, like those found in England. The boys in Breslau, for example, learned the alphabet, the Lord's Prayer, the Hail Mary, Creed, Psalter, and singing, and studied Latin grammar in the well-known books. The earliest departures from tradition were naturally seen in the city schools of Italy, which, like the German, began in the thirteenth century. There had always been more freedom in Italy. Private schools had for a long time been known: that is to say, schools set up by private masters, clerks, not laymen, with the licence to teach. It is probable that the existence of these schools had something to do with the development of the schools in great cities like Genoa and Florence, where in later times we may find guilds of masters, admitting new members and themselves giving the licence to teach, and municipal control; but we have also to remember the urban traditions of Italian life, in accounting for the spread of city schools, supported by the city and town authorities. The Italian universities themselves were in much closer touch, especially in financial matters, with the city than universities ever were, or could be, in other countries. Naturally enough, in these Italian schools the instruction was more free: just as we find more laymen, like the great Dante, attending the cathedral schools, even the schools of theology, so we find more elasticity in the city schools. The merchants wanted their sons to learn grammar and the *abacus* and to have more technical instruction; and generally they wished them to go into their counting-houses and become merchants in their turn. In an atmosphere of this kind, good keen teachers might go far and anticipate the spirit of the great humanist teachers, who are often erroneously regarded as the founders of our modern educational life.

The material surroundings in medieval schools were, as a rule, not good. It is not likely that they would be better than they were in the universities, although they would frequently be more quiet. As we read of the physical difficulties under which teachers taught in the famous University of Paris—the noise, stench, confinement—we may well wonder how such great work as they did was ever done. It was doubtless the sense of the contrast between what was and what might be which made a well-known teacher in Italy in the early thirteenth century write an account of the ideal schoolroom. Buoncompagno is said to have had five hundred pupils, and he had not been very comfortable. This is what he would have liked:

'A school house built in fresh pure air, far from the concourse of women, the cries of the market-place, the neighing of horses, and the barking of dogs, from shipping, from harmful gossip, from the squeaking of carts and from smells. A good number of windows, with neither too much nor too little light, but as nature herself requires. A school room (*habitaculum*) on an upper floor, with a roof not too high nor lying too near the floor, for each of these defects hampers the working of the memory. It should be cleaned of all dust and dirt, with no pictures save perhaps those which fix in the memory forms and figures relating to the studies on which the mind is engaged: the walls painted green and only one door and easy stairs. A master's seat set high so that he can see all who enter; two or three windows so placed that, especially in fine weather, the master can see trees and gardens and orchards, for the memory is strengthened by the sight of pleasant things. The scholars' seats so arranged that everyone can see the master easily. . . . Everyone to sit in order and not to change his place.'

He ends:

'I never had a house built like this, nor do I think that such has ever been built anywhere. But this idea of mine may perhaps be of some use to those who come after me.'

Buoncompagno was teaching people who were gradually becoming organized as students in universities—men from different countries, and varying much in age, standing, and ability. But I imagine that the conditions and needs in humble schools were much the same. The teacher did not read his lectures—Buoncompagno speaks of the importance of memory—and in all schools, as now, except that modern children have books, teaching was in rapid *viva voce*; great stress in the teaching of young children was laid on repetition. The classes in city schools seem to have been large, often from 60 to 100; a Florentine chronicler, writing soon after 1300, says that there were from eight to ten thousand scholars in Florence, and if he was right, nearly one-tenth of the population must have gone to the Florentine schools. But Florence was always an exceptional place.

Buoncompagno, when he speaks of the lighting of windows, says that the light should be as nature requires. This was a frequent phrase in the writings of medieval experts on education. Art, says Dante, follows nature as the scholar follows his master in repetition. It is nature that does the work in a healthy mind—for the teacher, as St. Thomas Aquinas taught, is the servant of nature. For this reason, medieval writers lay so much stress on the relations between masters and pupils, and on moral discipline, for knowledge is but a means to an end—a means to wisdom—and the passage from knowledge to wisdom is not easy nor direct; goodness must lie between. To be wise, men must be in harmony with the nature of things, and all things, when they follow their nature, follow the law of their being, which comes from God.

A great deal more than this could be said about medieval education. Like everything else, it was no doubt very unsatisfactory, whether compared by medieval standards or by ours. But I hope that I have said enough to suggest to you that we may learn something from it.

V

SOME PROBLEMS IN THE HISTORY OF THE MEDIEVAL UNIVERSITY[1]

THE questions which, I imagine, are most frequently asked about the medieval university run something like this: What was the value of all this intellectual activity? Was there any sequence or permanence in it? What kind of degree did scholars take? Was it a mere form, or did it involve a serious mental discipline? We can best get some ideas about the answers to such questions—I do not say that we can ever get very satisfying answers—by looking at Paris in the middle of the fourteenth century.

By this time the University was fully developed. The four faculties of Arts, Medicine, Decrees, and Theology were clearly defined, each with its own statutes, organization, and records. Three of them, if not all four, were localized, that is to say, their studies and activities went on in definite areas of the university quarter. Just as at Bologna the jurists had their head-quarters in the Dominican and the artists in the Franciscan church, so the artists in Paris lived in the neighbourhood of the church of St. Julian and in the Rue du Fouarre, while the decretists or canonists lived in the Clos Brunel. The use which the theologians made of the College of Robert de Sorbon was in all probability the result of a similar tendency, especially among the secular theologians,[2] though it would be as wrong to identify the Faculty of Theology in the Middle Ages with the Sorbonne as to identify the jurists of Bologna with the Dominicans. The Faculty of Medicine, always more closely connected with the Faculty of Arts, appears to have had

[1] An address given to the Royal Historical Society, 8 February 1934.

[2] The University used the Sorbonne for disputations from at least the early years of the fourteenth century; see the *Chartularium*, ii. 693, with Denifle's note, p. 695. The *Sorbonica* or disputation, held on Saturdays between members of the College, was carefully regulated in 1344. The statutes issued by the *provisor* of the College in this year suggest that this domestic exercise was a new departure, different from the disputations mentioned in the university statutes (*Chartularium*, ii. no. 1096).

no definite centre; it is not known to have acquired a home until 1470 when it bought a house in the Rue de la Bucherie. But its precious commentaries, or records of Faculty meetings, survive from the year 1395, and its distinct organization under a Dean can be traced back at least to 1330. Each Faculty, and each of the four Nations which together made up the Faculty of Arts, had its parchment book of statutes, privileges, and calendar, and its continuous paper registers which contained the minutes of meetings, and the names of scholars admitted as bachelors, or to the licence and the full mastership. The registers of the Anglo-German Nation survive from 1332—a very precious record of academic activity from month to month in one society or corporation of the university. Until the commentaries of the Medical Faculty begin in 1395, and the registers of the Faculty of Decrees in 1414, they are the only record of the kind. Sometimes the registers tell us about meetings of Congregation, the assembly of masters of all faculties. But the more important proceedings of Congregation were described in reports and memoranda which, though sometimes they survive separately, are for the most part found in one or more of the chartularies of the university: and these chartularies seem to have been compiled as often for the use of nations and faculties as for the use of university officials as such.

Congregation might include as many as 200 masters; it usually met at St. Mathurin. No doubt customary meeting-places came in time to be used by the several nations and faculties; but there was no fixed rule. The English Nation, for example, met in many different places, including the houses of officials and on at least one occasion in a tavern. The examinations *in camera*, which preceded the formal rites of inception or the licence, were apparently held anywhere, just as in our universities to-day examiners sometimes conduct oral examinations, discuss the written questions or decide the fate of candidates in private houses or college rooms. Official life in the University of Paris was not merely a series of solemn acts directed by solemn bedels, of formal public meetings and elaborate religious ceremonies, or of feasts and junketings. It was the life of men who did a great deal of academic work in informal ways. These men were crowded together in colleges, hospices, houses, and lodgings. The 'scholars' comprised men and boys of different ages and dignity and social importance. One gets the impression that the gradual passage from the status of scholar to that of bachelor and of bachelor to master was not the orderly affair which it is to-day, but might be accompanied by great discomfort; it was not easy to find *scolæ* or rooms for the exercises of the bachelors; men qualified for the licence might have to wait a long time and to use arts and blandishments to get it; masters could not be sure of finding a school in which to teach. This aspect of the medieval university has not been systematically studied and perhaps will always be a matter of surmise. We can learn a good deal about forms and constitutions on the one hand, and of the less academic sides of student life on the other; but so far we can only form impressions about the heat, the intensity, the personal give and take of everyday academic life. Yet this was the real life of the university, for in this combination of routine and scramble the masters and scholars gave or heard lectures, conducted or attended disputations, and found time and place for private study; it was in this atmosphere that they took sides on all the vexed questions of the day, from the casual incidents of a crowded and in every sense a very touchy companionship to the larger matters of academic prestige, public concern, theological or philosophical controversy, and high ecclesiastical policy.

The labour of recent scholars upon the manuscripts which contain the writings of scholastics—both the great men and those of secondary importance—has given the intellectual life of Paris a new perspective. It helps to give us a clearer impression of a closely knit, if turbulent, actually society alive and carried along by its own impetus. We cannot realize the significance of a medieval university if we do not go beyond a classification of its activities and a summary description of its interests. Let me illustrate this point by a few definite considerations:

1. The university was intensely self-conscious and self-important. To what extent this was true of other univer-

sities requires investigation, but it was true of Paris and Bologna. The graduates of Paris were scattered over Europe and did not forget their colleagues at the *alma mater*. The regent masters felt that they were the centre and source of the intellectual life of Europe, the spring of the *Studium* which refreshed the *Imperium* and the *Sacerdotium*, and was one of the three functions of the Christian society. When the project of a Council was under discussion during the Schism, the theologians and decretists of Paris insisted that the representatives of law and theology should equal in numbers the representatives of the hierarchy and monastic orders. Their arrogance shocked some of those who shared their conciliar views. Dietrich of Niem, for example, protested against it. Now this spirit was no new thing; it was merely an expression of an habitual attitude of mind, the attitude rebuked by the future Boniface VIII in November 1290, when, as Papal legate, he trounced the academic critics of Pope Martin IV's privilege in favour of mendicant orders. Certain masters had determined against the bull: he would have them know that the feet of the church were *non plumeos sed plumbeos*. 'You sit in chairs and think that Christ is ruled by your reasonings.' One is reminded of Harnack's remark about the professors of Berlin, that they thought they sat at the loom of history. The confidence of the Parisian masters in themselves was not unnatural. It had been fostered by flattery and protection, and was kept lively by constant disputes over the judicial immunities of the Parisian scholars. During one of these disputes, a master seriously suggested that both the bishop and the provost of Paris as *conservator* of the university should be summoned before Congregation as before a tribunal. During a controversy (1384) about the right of the canons of Notre-Dame to lecture on the canon law, the decretists maintained their claim to monopoly by elaborate historical arguments and by dwelling upon the advantages which concentrated study and teaching in a closely confined area possessed over the more leisurely and isolated performances of a clergyman in a cathedral close. Here we come to the heart of the matter.

2. The masters, we have seen, had discussed the bull of

Martin IV in their lecture rooms. They had weighed the pros and cons and had 'determined' upon them. The *scola* was indeed the workshop of opinion; it was an intellectual smithy, to which metal of every kind could be brought. One of the hottest disputes of the fourteenth century (1385) concerned the duties of the chancellor towards bachelors who had qualified for the licence. The masters claimed that the real work was done by them: they examined the candidates and gave the necessary certificates; they decided who should or should not have the licence to teach. It was the duty of the chancellor not to discriminate or delay or accept large gifts which in reality were bribes. And the chancellor complained that one master had 'determined' that he was a heretic, for he was obstinate in the breach of his sworn trust and so was rejecting the divinely disposed order of things. The appeal to the schools was no formality in the Middle Ages. When Thomas Cranmer, then a theological master at Cambridge, suggested that King Henry VIII should refer the problem of the divorce to the Universities, he was not merely suggesting a way out of a difficulty. He was influenced by a tradition which had been immensely strengthened by use since, more than 250 years before, another King Henry had played with the idea of submitting his dispute with Thomas Becket to the judgement of the masters of Paris. Almost anything might be referred to the judgement of the masters. Their deliberations upon matters of ecclesiastical, theological, moral, and public interest would fill many large volumes.[1]

In matters of heresy the joint commissions of theologians and the local authority, including the inquisitor, came to have executive authority in Northern France. And the schools where the masters lectured or presided over disputations were the workshops of the opinion, which was expressed in solemn judgements of the University. I am inclined to think that the preoccupation of historians with the general trend of medieval thought and particularly with the work of the Dominicans and Franciscans has tended

[1] e.g. the sentences of censure pronounced by the Faculty of Theology before 1735 fill the three folio volumes of the *Collectio judiciorum de novis erroribus*, made by the Bishop of Tulle, C. du Plessis d'Argentré (Paris 1724–36; new edition, 1755).

to conceal the significance of this fact. Although another favourite preoccupation of medieval scholars is the organic nature of medieval society, with its estates, corporations, and gilds, the activity of the University as a social structure has been overlooked. In the medieval section of his well-known book, *Die Soziallehren der christlichen Kirchen*, Ernst Troeltsch omits altogether any consideration of the Universities as such. Now it is true enough that, in the thirteenth century, the Dominicans and Franciscans set the pace in the development of scholasticism, but the treatment of this fact in historical literature conveys a very misleading impression of academic life.[1] The Dominican priory at Paris, for example, was not a kind of beneficent cancer which absorbed the life of the university and drained the secular element of vitality. What happened was something like this. Two great centres of intellectual activity were fostered, partly by their own internal energy, partly by papal support and direction. One of them, the University of Paris, was centralized; the other, the system of Dominican schools, was a kind of distributed university, highly organized, pervading the whole order. Much of the more important work of St. Thomas was not lectured and written at Paris at all, but in the Italian *studia* of his order. The two movements naturally had to find a *modus vivendi* at the point where they met: the danger that the Dominican (and, a lesser danger, that the Franciscan) theologians might secure a monopoly was for a time a real one, especially as it coincided with a crisis in the history of the Parisian schools, but, once surmounted, it and other problems incidental to the presence of flourishing Mendicant priories were adjusted—uneasily, unevenly, with all the clamour and publicity which attend academic disputes—but they were adjusted. And in the process of adjustment each side strengthened the other. The mendicant philosophers and theologians had in Paris a sounding-board. The secular masters learned something from the organization of the new orders and got prestige from the fame of some of their new

[1] In his *Répertoire des maîtres en théologie de Paris au XIIIe siècle* (Paris, 1933), Father P. Glorieux deals with 71 Dominican and 233 secular masters of theology. In a forthcoming section he will deal with 51 Franciscan masters.

colleagues. St. Thomas, at Paris, like the Franciscan John Pecham at Oxford, probably put some method into the traditional system of disputations. But nobody at Paris in the thirteenth and fourteenth centuries would recognize the conventional picture of the medieval university in that city as the home of a few great men, followers of St. Francis and St. Dominic, surrounded by a crowd of garrulous dullards. This is a ridiculous travesty of the truth.

3. The intensive work, to which I have referred, upon the manuscripts of this period has done much to recapture the activity of the schools and to rehabilitate the secular masters. It has shown that the text-books—what we call 'set books'—were the occasion of incessant discussion, so that there was gradually accumulated about them in the stationers' shops an important lending library of accredited commentaries and treatises. Each faculty had its prescribed texts,[1] just as the theologians had the Bible and the Sentences of that very great man Peter the Lombard. Rashdall was puzzled by the *ars medicinae*; he thought it was a book, whereas we now know that it was a *corpus* of texts, originally due to the famous teacher of Salerno, Constantinus Africanus, who lived in the eleventh century—a group of medical texts which medical students had to know. The artists had their exegetic lectures on logical and Aristotelean texts; they had lectures in the course of which 'disputed questions' were dealt with under the careful guidance of the master and his bachelor; they had sophistical disputations, corresponding, as Monsignor Grabmann has pointed out, to the *quodlibets* of the theologians, in which, according to fixed rules, all sorts of matters could be fully discussed and disputed, before the presiding master summed up and determined. The decretists had the Decretum of Gratian and the Decretals of Gregory IX, Boniface VIII, and Clement V, masters lecturing on the Decretum, bachelors on the rest. In the Faculty of Theology the bachelors lectured on the Sentences, while the masters did the greater part of the teaching and lecturing on the Scrip-

[1] The late Stephen d'Irsay's *Histoire des Universités* (Paris, 1933), vol. i, although it adds nothing to our knowledge of university organization, rightly emphasizes this side of university life.

tures. Most of the surviving literature was clearly based on this teaching, or records these disputations, and most of the literature which does not reflect this experience was intended for the use of teachers and scholars. The catalogues of libraries, notably of the Sorbonne early in the fourteenth century, show conclusively that the University of Paris was much more than a society of boys who read a few text-books, of disputes which led nowhere, and of a few exceptional men who worked aloof from the life around them.

4. Time has done rough justice to this mass of learning. The wheat has been separated from the chaff. But the toilers of to-day, as they work among the chaff, have discovered many precious things. Much of it remains pure chaff. Indeed, when all this work is done, I imagine that its main value will be in the revelation of that continuous activity, in which the grain was sown from generation to generation, and the sowers were disciplined to scatter it—and a lot of chaff with it—at the call of popes and kings, councils, bishops, inquisitors, or to carry it away—a source of inward sustenance rather than of outward influence—in the service of the Church and State.

Yet this is by no means the whole story. Perhaps the best illustration of the point which I am trying to make is to be found in the history of logic. At first sight nothing is less helpful. We are told, for example, that a Durham man, William Shirewood, much praised by Roger Bacon, had great reputation as a teacher of logic at Paris; that one of his pupils, Petrus Hispanus, later Pope John XXI (1276), compiled a text-book of logic, the *Summulae logicales* which was destined to be for centuries the favourite text-book in the subject; that in succession to him we find important logicians, among them John Buridan, who was rector of the university in 1327 and 1348 and wrote important commentaries on the *Physics* and other Aristotelean works. This does not take us very far; but if we can trust the experts, we have here the bare bones of a significant story. Peter Hispanus summed up a stage in the development of dialectic—the dialectic of the sophistical disputations in which the sceptics and Averroists of the thirteenth century, headed by Siger of Brabant, found expression. We find this dialectic flourishing early in the next century at Oxford, and though its work was soon forgotten in England, it lived on the continent, where the names of Oxford scholars, much distorted by foreign lips, were to be familiar in the Italian schools until the beginning of the seventeenth century. Meanwhile, logical exercises in Paris had been more fruitful; dialectical method was used, on the one hand, in the interpretation of Aristotelean science, on the other, to explain the direct observation of natural phenomena: the outcome was the teaching of Buridan and his followers. Their theories of physics, especially Buridan's theory of *impetus*, in due course influenced the great Italian scientists of the sixteenth century, who were not so independent of their predecessors as is generally supposed. In other words, modern science does not start with Leonardo da Vinci, Galileo, and the rest; it began at Paris in the classrooms and studies in the crowded narrow streets of the artists' quarter, and the way to it was prepared by men, young and old, who had wrangled about logical terms and pored over the text of Aristotle and had gradually realized how important it was to observe facts for themselves.

Buridan was an Occamist, one of many. He did not hold with the 'moderns', as they were called, the extremists among the later Occamists who denied that the existence of God could be proved; but he and his successors, in what are often believed to be the barren years, were deep in those discussions about names and things which were to affect the history of the modern world.

There seems no reason to doubt that this period saw a turning-point in the history of thought. At bottom the issue between the Thomists and the new nominalism (and how recently the teaching of St. Thomas had itself been suspect) turned upon the possibility of believing in the essential reasonableness of the universe. If faith need not be divorced from reason, conscience need not be in a state of civil war, divided against itself; the sanctions of behaviour, whether political or religious, are not capable of fundamental discord. This is the Thomist view. But the Occamist philosophy, reflecting and justifying current tendencies, was different. Luther, who read the Occamists, and perhaps did not always understand them, was tortured by a sense of discord which he could not transcend. That facts were not in harmony might be transitory, but there was a fundamental lack of coherence in intellectual experience. A man, while intent on personal salvation, might have a duty, a moral duty, to sin in maintaining the sanctions of society and the state. The brutal instinct which sends a criminal to be broken on the wheel has its own authority. Luther's successors, and men and women in all countries, are face to face with this dreadful dilemma to-day.

In these notes on Paris in the fourteenth century I have said enough, I hope, to show that the first questions with which I began are serious questions: 'What was the value of all this intellectual activity? Was there any sequence or permanence in it?' And the next two questions, 'What kind of degree did scholars take? Was it a mere form, or did it involve a serious mental discipline?' are clearly very serious questions also. The point to be made here is that, in such an academic life as I have tried to suggest existed in Paris, intellectual earnestness and excellence were not revealed by a kind of accident; they were not in the nature of the case exceptional. They were encouraged. A keen student found incentive all about him. This after all is the main thing. It would be absurd to suppose that the students in the medieval university were, as a whole, an especially bright or conscientious set of men, though I imagine that circumstances selected them quite as carefully as they select university students to-day. As a medieval distich says: 'You may send a little donkey to Paris, but if he is an ass here, he won't be a horse there.' Whatever he were, he could find plenty of fodder. Rashdall, who was the last man to encourage any illusion on this subject, points out that the obligation to attend and, later, to take part in disputations, deprives the problem of efficiency in examinations of much of its significance.[1] A

[1] Rashdall, i. 471; cf. 456 *seqq.* Since this paper was written, the publication of the volume of *Oxford Theology and Theologians, c. 1282–1302*, by A. G. Little and F. Pelster (Oxford Historical Society, vol. xcvi, Oxford, 1934), has greatly facilitated the understanding of the academic exercises at Paris and Oxford; see pp. 29–56.

young man who had 'determined' in arts, or a theologian who had reached the grade of 'formed bachelor', had gone through a very severe discipline. The determiner, for example, had been required to display intellectual agility and persistence in disputations which lasted for several weeks. The formed bachelor had been required to lecture on the Sentences and knew that if his lectures, when he had revised and published them, won esteem, his name would be made. The very conditions which would help a scholar to be idle or perfunctory, could encourage another to put out all his powers. Until 1452 lectures in arts and, both before and after 1452, lectures in law were given without notes and in a rapid or at least continuous voice, without pauses. A good lecturer had to be quite sure of himself and a good hearer had to have a retentive memory. There was a great to-do in the Faculty of Decrees in 1386 when a master, usurping the function of the bachelors, lectured to large and profitable audiences on the Decretals by the light of a candle, that is to say, read lectures which could be taken down. These particular lectures according to the statutes had always to be given by a bachelor at an early hour; no candle was allowed, and as the academic year comprised the period when the days were short, this meant that the lectures were given in darkness. Although the masters presumably lectured in daylight, it must have been very difficult to take their lectures down—a fact which may even help to explain the discrepancies and incoherences in the *reportationes* or texts made by the masters' bachelors. Now when we remember that these lectures were full of references, we realize that they might put a heavy strain upon the attention and memory of those who heard them. The relations between master and pupil and the importance of the memory in the medieval system of education are described very neatly in a short tract, *De regimine et modo studendi*, written in the thirteenth century by an Italian master, Martino da Fano. The tract is dedicated to his pupils (*dilectissimis scolaribus*). He advises them, in their judgement of a master, to consider whether he teaches the things which he ought to teach, is willing to answer questions, and draws out what is in the inquirer's mind. Does he suffer opposition sensibly and give reasons for what he asserts? Does he make an adequate impression upon his hearers and use effective illustrations to explain his arguments? Is he free from pretentiousness, really helpful, and more concerned with the truth than with fine tricks of speech? Then, turning to the scholars, Martin warns them to set a high standard before themselves, to see that they understand the legal argument so that everything fits and not to think they know unless they fully understand every part. 'And finally, as you lie in bed or walk about the street, go over what you have learned and say, "To-day I have learned so many laws, and these are the opening words of each."'[1] Again, some of you will remember the story of Albert the Great, how while he was lecturing one day in his *scola* at Cologne his memory suddenly failed him and his reasoning would not come. He sat silent for a little while: then, flushed and comforted, he told his pupils that the Virgin had appeared to him long ago, and after she had anticipated a life of great learning for him, had warned him that this would happen to him, *in publico officio lectionis*. From this time he gave himself to prayer, and, though he could still remember his texts, the power to recollect *rationes philosophicae* never returned to him.

He could still remember his texts. One version of the story defines this as the text of scripture and philosophy, though what the content of *philosophia* was I do not know. The implication is that Albert knew the Bible and a good deal of Aristotle by heart. If this is not interpreted pedantically, I imagine that it is true. A true medieval scholar knew the great texts of his subject and could refer to them from memory. Now any one who has ever looked at a medieval commentary or a reading (*lectura*) in the civil or canon law can realize the significance of this fact. It suggests a mental discipline as astonishing to us as the physical discipline suggested by a suit of medieval armour. Picture to yourselves a young law student attending a lecture in the dark, a lecture given in a level continuous voice, without pauses. Picture him later, as a bachelor, engaged in disputations or

[1] Edited by L. Frati, in *Studi e Memorie per la Storia dell'Università di Bologna* (1926), vi, 25–9.

in lecturing on the problems raised by a decretal. Think of the opponent ready to trip him up and on the alert for the least slip. A man who could go through this discipline and be certified as ready to undergo an examination *in camera* might well be permitted to pass on to his mastership after a very perfunctory test. I do not deny that there were ways of evasion and periods of slack administration; but, so far as I can understand the texts, the system was more or less as I have sketched it. In any case, before we safely conclude that every one passed his examination as a matter of course, we must know two things: first, how many scholars dropped out by the way; secondly, are the records, even when they seem to be complete, records of successful candidates only, or of all candidates, all of whom got through?

The impression that medieval examinations can be ignored is untrue, and results from a hasty concentration on the more formal ceremonies, which fill so much space in the university statutes. The belief in a course of apprenticeship, followed by testing, is fundamental in early societies, as we may learn from the anthropologists, as well as from Tacitus and the practices of medieval chivalry, and of medieval arts and crafts. The examination system is very old and in the Middle Ages was widespread. There is a story of an examination in medicine at Salerno about 1200, when a rejected candidate went in disgust to Montpellier. Stray references in Buoncompagno's writings seem to imply examinations at Bologna about the same time, and the letters of Pope Honorius III to the archdeacon of Bologna enforced them. Grabmann has noted in two thirteenth-century manuscripts a collection of questions to be discussed in examinations on the Arts course at Paris together with the answers. At the Papal Court poor petitioners for benefices had to undergo examinations, and records of the reports of examiners survive, saying how one candidate sang badly, or another failed to satisfy in reading. It should be noted, by the way, that university graduates were excused this examination, and the fourteenth-century university graduates in the main depended upon the Pope for provision to benefices. Our chief record of the graduates of Paris and Oxford, for example, is the *rotuli* containing the names of graduates submitted by the authorities to the Papal Court; and when the withdrawal of obedience at Paris during the Papal Schism, and the Statutes of Provision and Praemunire in England, seemed likely to interfere with the transmission of the *rotuli*, the consternation in university circles was very great. But my point is that at the Papal Court graduation in a university was considered to be a proof of competence; it excused applicants for papal provisions from examination.

In the statutes of the theological faculty at Bologna, edited by the late Cardinal Ehrle, we have precise regulations for examination. The statutes were compiled in 1364 and were explicitly based on those of Paris, which are now lost. Here is the statute headed 'on the procedure to be observed in the private examination'. The candidates were bachelors who had been recommended for admission to the test which preceded the conferment of the licence, i.e. the mastership or doctorate in theology. I summarize the text: As effort wanes without reward, so distinction suffers if it is given to the unworthy. It is inconsistent with our duty to acquiesce in either of these possibilities, so we prescribe as follows. Three days before the examination the dean shall choose two subjects (*puncta*), that is, two *distinctiones* from the Sentences. He shall frame two very debatable questions, suggested by these, stating both sides of the case, and shall give these in writing to the candidate. A full day before the examination (i.e. two days later) the candidate shall give in writing to each master in the faculty his reasoned conclusions on each question, under four or five heads. On the next day at the eighteenth hour those masters whose schools are incorporated in the theological body (*universitas*) shall come together in conclave before the chancellor. First the dean, then each master in turn, according to seniority, shall dispute against the position taken by the candidate on the first *questio*, giving two or three reasoned arguments, which are to be sprung upon the candidate, or as we say, to be 'unseen'. The candidate must give three reasoned replies (*replicationes*) to the first argument and two to the second. And then the same process is to be observed in dealing with the position on the other *questio*. When all this is over, the candidate shall be sent out of the room, and the chancellor shall call on each master to give his honest opinion both of the moral character of the candidate and of his fitness for the degree. (In 1364 the decision of the weightier—*major vel sanior*—element prevailed ; according to a later recension of the statutes the voting was by ballot and three adverse votes could fail the candidate.) Until his success is assured the candidate must on no account, on pain of perjury, offer gifts to his examiners ; but later he may offer them wine and refreshment, provided that the cost of the entertainment does not exceed two florins. I doubt if I could ever have passed an examination of this kind.

VI
GERALD OF WALES[1]

THE career of Gerald of Wales suggests some striking reflections to the student of our early history. He lives, and lives vigorously, only in his own writings, some of which survive only in one manuscript. If these works had been lost, as so much medieval literature has been lost, we should know almost nothing about him. A troublesome archdeacon, chosen by his fellow canons as bishop of St. David's, a man whose 'rebel cleverness' caused much trouble at the papal court to a hard-worked Archbishop of Canterbury—that is about all; he would have been one among many troublesome archdeacons, and claimants to bishoprics and persistent suitors at Rome. Scholars, I imagine, would have speculated mildly about the identity of the 'Gerald the archdeacon' who attested here and there an Anglo-Irish charter; they could never have felt the pleasant thrill of recognition, as they note the presence of the vivacious ecclesiastic who wrote the most famous of all the famous books about Ireland.

Of course, there is nothing new, though there is always something strange, in this. If Pepys had never written a diary or if his diary had been lost, he would have been known to us only as a very intelligent and reasonably hard-working official of the Admiralty. If Greville had not written a diary he would not be known at all except as Clerk to the Privy Council; and, as you are aware, some extremely interesting and spicy diaries, published for the first time in recent years, were written by persons so unknown to history that their authenticity has been doubted, just as the authenticity of the Paston Letters was long discussed until their consistency with other historical evidence was established. Yet there is something peculiarly suggestive about the nature of our knowledge of Gerald. Whatever value we attach to his statements, there is no doubt that he was in

[1] A lecture given in the John Rylands Library, 11 January 1928. I am indebted to Mr. Richard Hunt for some corrections.

his way a very important man, a man who could not fail to attract attention and arouse comment. He did not live obscurely; he was not one of those people whose personality seems only to be revealed in their writings; he was not, like Hobbes, a retiring and rather timid soul, who could show an unexpected, devastating courage on paper, or, like Sir Isaac Newton, a man whose commonplace life was but the tabernacle of a mind really at home with the infinite. His writings are not like the poetry of Dante or Shakespeare, so packed with the experience and strivings of humanity that contact with the daily lives of the writers is lost or becomes a trivial impertinence. Gerald lived in the open. His life was full of public activity, his interests were those of every day. He was familiar with kings and could banter with popes. He was an aristocrat inordinately proud of his lineage, a self-important gossip whom nothing escaped. He was a scholar who could only do lip-service to the charms of retirement, a man with intense curiosity and uncannily observant, ever ready to speculate about the origin of things, the peculiarities of custom or the meaning of words. He loved preaching and lecturing, and he revelled in controversy. He had unbounded courage, preferred to fight with the great, and his self-esteem was never disturbed by the frustrations of what we call self-consciousness. He knew everybody and went everywhere. Yet, if it were not for his writings, we should know next to nothing about him. The significance of a fact such as this should never be forgotten by students of early history, embarrassed though they may be by the wealth of the scattered and scrappy material at their disposal. It reminds us very forcibly that the growth of English law and society, the development of our ecclesiastical and political institutions, were not supervised by mechanical despots ruling over a crowd of dummies, but were the living expressions of living people, far too much interested in what they and others were doing to trouble much about where they were going or to trouble at all about us.

Gerald's writings fill eight volumes of the Rolls Series. The editorial work is of varying merit, that of Dr. Brewer being especially defective. Brewer's edition of the autobiography and of parts of the 'Invectives' appeared so long ago as 1861. A recent edition of the 'Invectives', issued by Mr. W. S. Davies in a volume of *Y Cymmrodor* (1920), has done something to fill the gaps in Brewer's work. It is unlikely that much more can be done with profitable results until the intensive studies, now in full progress, in the literary, social, and ecclesiastical history of the twelfth century can be brought to bear upon Gerald's multifarious writings.

A strong autobiographical interest inspired all the best work of Gerald. He could never get away from himself for very long, and he is always most amusing and most helpful when he is writing from his own experience. He is induced, for example, or perhaps commissioned, to write the lives of Remigius, the first Norman bishop of Lincoln, and of his great contemporary, St. Hugh of Lincoln; he cannot resist the temptation to add little sketches, full of personal reminiscence, of other contemporary prelates. He writes a letter of encouragement to Archbishop Stephen Langton; but he goes off at a tangent to rail against a Canterbury monk who has attacked one of his books. Hence it is impossible to separate his writings from the incidents of his life.

The books on Wales and Ireland are connected with Gerald's early life. They are the works by which he was best known in his own day and is best known to-day; for they broke new ground and are still alive as historical material. Indeed, the 'Topography of Ireland' has been for centuries one of the storm centres in the disputes about the nature and value of early Irish society. One of the most solid productions of the literary activity which accompanied the nationalist movements in Ireland in the seventeenth century was the *Cambrensis Eversus* of the Roman Catholic refugee, John Lynch (1662). If Irish history was to be properly understood, the authority of the Welshman must be overthrown. The controversy has not yet ceased. Now Gerald's work was due to the fact that he was closely related to a Norman family, settled in Pembrokeshire, which took a large share in the conquest of southern Ireland. He was a Pembrokeshire man, and on his father's side he was a Norman, on his mother's side half a Norman. Hence, although at times Gerald liked to boast of his Welsh ancestry, it is more correct to describe him as Gerald de Barri, son of William de Barri, or as Gerald of Wales than as Gerald the Welshman. His grandfather Odo was one of the foreign settlers who (in the reign of King Henry I) occupied the district known as southern Dyfed. He was succeeded about 1130 by his son William, Gerald's father. The family seat was the castle of Manorbier (Maenor Pŷr or Bŷr), the ruins of which still remain, looking out over the Bristol Channel, a few miles to the south-east of Pembroke. It is a very pleasant place, and in Gerald's eyes it was the most beautiful place in Wales. He wrote in later years of the park and fishpond, and the lovely orchard, and the rivulet of never-failing water which flowed down between the castle and the church. As a boy he had watched the ships being driven by an east wind to Ireland. 'Demetia is the fairest district in Wales, and Pembroke the fairest part of it, and this the fairest spot in Pembroke; it follows that Maenor Pŷr is the most pleasant spot in Wales. Let the writer be excused for saying so much in praise of his birthplace.'[1]

William, the lord of Manorbier, married the daughter of a local magnate, an important man in himself, and still more important as the ancestor of one of the greatest of the Anglo-Irish families. This was Gerald of Windsor, constable of Pembroke, and through his son, the famous Maurice fitz Gerald, the ancestor of the Geraldines, Earls of Kildare. Gerald of Windsor had married a Welsh princess, and it was through their daughter Angharad, the wife of William de Barri, that Gerald of Wales was able to claim descent from the Kings of South Wales. The princess, Nest or Nesta, daughter of King Rhys ap Tewdwr, had an exciting career. She was twice married, first to Gerald of Windsor, then to the constable of Cardigan; and for some

[1] It is hard to find a translation for *maenor*, which usually means an administrative sub-district. Here it may mean the chieftain's vill. The court-house or *mansio* was generally in the lord's bond-vill in the commote or wider district (W. Rees, *South Wales and the March*, p. 303). Maenor Pŷr is said to be the maenor of the lords, *pŷr* being the plural of the old Welsh word *por*, a lord; but Professor Rees, who has kindly sent me notes on this paper, thinks that there is a good deal to be said for Gerald's derivation 'mansio Pirri' (vi. 92), i.e. that Pŷr is a personal name, possibly the equivalent of Porius.

time she was the mistress of King Henry I. She had children by all three, and nearly all her sons or grandsons were destined to have a share in the booty of Ireland. King Henry's grandson, Meiler fitz Henry, a strong little man with stern black eyes, was one of the first group of invaders, and in King John's reign became justiciar of Ireland. Of the three sons of Nesta and Gerald of Windsor, one was the founder of the Carews and two other Irish families; one, as we have seen, the ancestor of the Geraldines, a third, David, was bishop of the Welsh see of St. David's. They were the maternal uncles of Gerald of Wales. Robert fitz Stephen, the son of Nesta and the constable of Cardigan, described by Gerald as a burly, healthy, jovial and generous man, too fond of women and wine, and—a second Marius—the sport of Fortune, was the leader of the first invaders and was granted the half of Cork. So we see that Gerald, who was a young man of twenty-three or twenty-four when his kinsmen made their bold expedition (1169), had access to the very heart of the turbulent politics of southern Wales and southern Ireland. In 1183 he accompanied his brother Philip to Ireland. In 1184 he was called to the court of King Henry II and was sent to Ireland in the following year in the company of the young John, the 'lord of Ireland'. The failure of John's expedition is well known. Gerald, whose sympathies would naturally lie with his kinsmen, the earliest invaders and settlers, ascribed it to the neglect of their advice and position and the presumptuous pressing forward of courtiers and new men who had no experience of the country. It is a cry often heard in the later history of Ireland. Gerald had no desire to settle. He refused the offer of several bishoprics, and stayed only long enough to collect the materials for his works on the conquest and on the topography of Ireland, which it appears were written before he left.

The main preoccupation of his life was found in Wales, and especially in the bishopric of St. David's, where his home and connexions were. He had made a reputation for himself in Wales long before he became a royal chaplain and accompanied the irresponsible young John to Ireland; and his interests were ecclesiastical. He tells in his autobiography how as a child he always played at churches while his brothers played at battles and castles; but these prophetic infantile preferences come in other people's lives, and Gerald saw his childhood through literary spectacles. He wanted to be a churchman and his uncle was the bishop of St. David's. After some years of study at the cathedral schools in Paris, he was ready for employment. In the year 1175 the new archbishop, Richard, sent him on a disciplinary mission to South Wales.[1] He was so effective that he was made archdeacon of Brecon and helped his old uncle, the bishop, to rule his diocese. Gerald was, as the Irish say, 'a bit of a lad'; he thoroughly enjoyed his work as archdeacon, and was especially proud of an encounter which he had with an old fellow student of his at Paris, the bishop of St. Asaph. The story is worth telling. Gerald had just returned home from a visitation of his mountainous and widespread district when he heard that the bishop proposed to dedicate a church at Kerry, on the border between the dioceses of St. Asaph and St. David's, but hitherto administered as part of the latter. He rushed off at once, and arrived in the neighbourhood on Saturday night, the eve of the ceremony. He had a number of clergy with him and had sent others for help in various directions. Like a good many Welsh churches in this period the church of St. Michael at Kerry was held jointly by more than one clerk, in this case by two, who had—against their will, they afterwards said—acquiesced in the invasion of episcopal authority from St. Asaph. They hid the keys of the church; but Gerald, arriving on Sunday morning, soon found them. The bells were rung in sign of possession and mass was said. In the meanwhile some of the bishop's clerks arrived with the parson (*persona*) to see that the church was ready for the dedication. Gerald sent off some of his clerks, together

[1] The chronology of Gerald's life, as told by himself, is characteristically inaccurate. Thus he says that he was present at the first public celebration of the feast of St. Thomas of Canterbury, celebrated two years after the martyrdom (vii. 69). This would be 29 Dec. 1172. But he also says that the archbishop, Richard, was present. There was no archbishop in Dec. 1172, and the first possible date is Dec. 1174, shortly after the archbishop's return from his consecration in Italy and also shortly after the destruction of the choir of the cathedral by fire. Gerald probably mixed up times, places, and persons. On the date of his mission to Wales see Lloyd, *History of Wales*, ii. 556, note.

with the rural dean, to learn the bishop's intentions and to offer him an honourable reception if he came in peace. The bishop was firm, and in spite of the dean's protest and appeal to the Pope, insisted on his right to perform the ceremony. Messengers were sent back to Gerald on swift horses, and the archdeacon took up a position to meet the usurper at the entrance to the cemetery. The bishop arrived and a long altercation began. Gerald, whose uncle, the bishop of St. David's, had recently died (1176), reminded his old friend and fellow student that the diocese was now in the custody of the king: the whole strength of the church and king in England was at his back. The bishop read out the letters received from the archbishop on his appointment to the see of St. Asaph, confirming him in *his* rights. The church of Kerry, he added, and all the churches between Wye and Severn in central Wales were within his jurisdiction. Literary evidence was also produced. Gerald retorted that anybody could write anything in a book. Where were the charters? Threats of excommunication were exchanged. The bishop said that an archdeacon could not excommunicate a bishop. Neither can a bishop, Gerald retorted, excommunicate an archdeacon who is not in his diocese.

'Hearing this, the bishop drew back a little, and on a sudden slipped from his horse and clapped on his mitre. Then mitre on head and staff in hand he advanced with his following, so that his sentence might be of greater effect. But the archdeacon knew the headstrong nature of the man. He had taken advantage of his garrulity to make his preparations and now ordered the clergy forward from the church. They wore white stoles and other ecclesiastical vestments and came in procession, with lighted candles and the cross borne in front of them.'

The bishop was taken aback, but announced that at least he would proceed to a general excommunication of all who resisted the rights of St. Asaph. Gerald pointed to the hills: 'Excommunicate on these mountains from dawn to dusk if you will—it will not hurt me,' but forbear, he added, lest you alarm and perplex the folk who have gathered about us. The bishop in a loud voice began to excommunicate; the archdeacon in a louder voice did the same. Then his eyes caught sight of the bells hanging behind him. He ordered a peal with triple interval to be rung in confirmation of his sentence. The bishop's assurance was broken —he rode away in confusion, and the people who had gathered raised a great shout against him and his companions, and pursued them with volleys of clods and missiles of wood and stone.

The whole of Gerald is in this story, told with his natural vigour and *naïveté*. The bishop was no less a person than Adam of Bangor, Adam of the Petit Pont, who had won fame as a teacher in his school on the bridge over the Seine at Paris. Gerald, a younger and less learned man, characteristically refers to him as a fellow student, and casts ridicule on his verbosity, his rashness, his humiliation. At no time was this son of Welsh kings and Norman barons a respecter of persons. We see his eye for detail, even in the absorption of a dispute on a solemn occasion: he suggests all the organization of the Church: pope, bishop, archdeacon, rural dean, parson, incumbents, clerks; he glances into the background of English power, vested in king and archbishop. He knows the effect of every detail in ritual, so that we see the lighted candles and hear the bells. He is in his wild Wales and his imagination turns instinctively to the neighbouring hills. Above all, he is after his rights, not so much his own as those of the office entrusted to him. Everything else is subsidiary to this. He is priest and scholar, but first and foremost he is the archdeacon, sure of his case, thorough, set on victory, disinterested yet fully aware of the fine impression which he, Gerald de Barri, is making. The story reached the ear of the king and caused much amusement at court, to Gerald's intense gratification. Disputes of this kind, grave or trivial, were occurring all over Europe. The record of them fills pages of papal registers and chronicles, and are in general very wearisome. The settlement of them helped to formulate the canon law or to define the relations between lay and clerical authority. Only now and then is the story given life. But Gerald lived every day an existence of dramatic egotism: and he wrote this and many more stories down, sometimes twenty years later, with the same zest as he had felt on the actual occasion. His memory was often at fault, but it never lacked colour.

In 1176, when his uncle died and these things happened, he was about thirty years of age, at the beginning of what seemed a brilliant career. In a later work he says that he was a very handsome young man. Once he visited two learned prelates and found them sitting together. One of them looked at Gerald and exclaimed 'Can such beauty die?' (iv. 104). Yet throughout his long life he never got further. He refused bishoprics in Wales and Ireland, and remained for many years an archdeacon in his native diocese of St. David's. It was in part his own fault, for he never made upon others the kind of impression which he made upon himself; but in part it was to his honour, for he was too big a man to have a merely vulgar ambition. You will have noticed that, at Kerry, he took the authority of king and archbishop in Wales for granted. He was at this time in the Anglo-Norman tradition. Archbishop Richard of Canterbury had sent him back to South Wales. But a new issue arose—a perplexing controversy which was to shape his later life, so that it obsessed his mind. This issue was the claim of the church of St. David's to archiepiscopal status, independent of the primacy of Canterbury. It had been raised in Henry I's reign, and on the death of Bishop David was revived in 1176. How Gerald regarded it at this time is uncertain. He was put forward precipitately by the canons as their chief candidate for the bishopric, and says that the archbishop wanted him; but the king refused, and the canons were told to elect a Cluniac, the prior of Wenlock in Shropshire. The election illustrates the attitude of Gerald at this time to the custom of England as described in the Constitutions of Clarendon, but his attitude to the problem of St. David's claims is not clear. He refused to be regarded as bishop-elect until the king's licence to elect had been given, and he acquiesced in his defeat with a good grace. If his later memory was sound, he was more concerned by the deplorable practice of electing a bishop in the king's private chamber than by any national feeling. St. Thomas had fought against this practice, but in vain. Gerald wanted to see things done in order: first, the king's licence, then a free election in the chapter. First by haste, in not waiting for the licence, then by fear, in choosing the royal nominee in the king's bedroom, the canons of St. David's had muddled matters. Yet the issue of St. David's status had been raised and was not forgotten, and it is quite probable that King Henry, in spite of his liking for Gerald and his pro-Welsh policy at this time, rejected him because he saw in him a possible danger as a protagonist of the local ambition. It was not only a racial ambition. It was indeed mainly ecclesiastical, based on a misunderstanding of documents and on memories of the independence of the old Celtic Church. A Norman ecclesiastic could share it as well as canons of Welsh blood; and Gerald, though I do not think that at this time he felt very strongly in the matter, was the sort of man to further it. At all events, the rebuff chafed him, and gradually he came to regard himself as a champion not only of canonical order but also of Welsh rights in the Church. The crisis came more than twenty years later. In 1177 Gerald went back to Paris; between 1180 and 1184 he was for some time engaged on work in the diocese of St. David's as the bishop's commissary; between 1189 and 1194 he was attached to the royal service and, in addition to his visit to Ireland in 1185–6, was constantly engaged during the troubled years after Henry II's death in delicate missions to the Welsh princes. He then withdrew from court. In 1196 he went to Lincoln to study under a famous scholar, William de Monte, then chancellor of Lincoln and in charge of the theological schools. In 1199 he was again put forward by the canons of St. David's, and in the long dispute which followed at the papal court his claim to the bishopric was inextricably connected with his assertion of the rights of the see to archiepiscopal dignity.

Nearly a quarter of a century (1176–99) had passed since Gerald had first been suggested as bishop. During the long interval Gerald's outlook on life had changed, I think, very considerably, and, quite apart from this—a matter of somewhat slight psychological interest—these were the most varied and interesting years in his life. His powers were developed and under control, and his best work belongs to this period. In his writings and later reminiscences we get a vivid picture of a busy-minded cleric, moving in the highest circles, political, ecclesiastical, literary, and ever at the heart of affairs.

Welsh problems engaged most of his attention. We may pass over his vain attempts to establish peace in the diocese of St. David's under the weak and querulous rule of its Cluniac bishop. The great event of the time was the fall of Jerusalem and the wave of indignant enthusiasm which led to the third crusade—the epic contest of Saladin and Richard of the Lion Heart. In 1188 Baldwin, archbishop of Canterbury, a Cistercian and a friend of Gerald's, planned a preaching tour in Wales on behalf of the crusade and took Gerald with him. Just as the visits to Ireland prompted his books on that country, so this tour hastened, if it did not prompt, his famous 'Itinerary' and his 'Description of Wales'. He had apparently planned his Description some time before, for, referring to its temporary loss during a journey from Normandy to England a year or so later, he describes it as the labour of many years and as yet existing in only one manuscript. It was actually finished and circulated when he was in Lincoln (*c.* 1195). The 'Itinerary' is his account of the preaching tour, of which he speaks also in his reminiscences. The archbishop's oratory was not effectual, but his own, he says, had a wonderful result. He did not speak Welsh—a point worth noting—and preached to the Welsh in French and Latin. Yet, just as St. Bernard, during his great Rhenish tour before the second crusade, had collected a host of German crusaders by his French sermons, Gerald's threatened to depopulate Wales, so great was the enthusiasm which they aroused for emigration to the East. One would like to know the facts behind this remarkable testimony. Gerald reports a conversation which he had later with John, to whom his father King Henry had given temporary control of the earldom of Pembroke before the succession of the young heiress. John, we are told, reproached Gerald, not for convincing Welshmen, but for depopulating Pembrokeshire of Normans, and grumbled that the archdeacon was plotting the return of the district to native rule. John had a strong sense of humour and, I suspect, was playing with Gerald. But Gerald took the accusation seriously and repudiated it. Here, at any rate, is a man of Welsh extraction, but not of Welsh race, who does not know Welsh, and is at the same time supposed to be infected by Welsh national sympathies. This sums up the position in 1188. Gerald at this time had obviously lost practical interest in the question of ecclesiastical independence, for he traversed Wales in the company of the Archbishop of Canterbury and raised no objection to Baldwin's insistence on the recognition of his supremacy by the Welsh chapters. During King Richard's absence in the East, he accepted commissions from John, from the queen mother and the temporary justiciar, Walter, Archbishop of Rouen, in furtherance of English policy in Wales. The power of the great king of South Wales, Rhys ap Gruffydd—Gerald's distant kinsman—was advancing during these years; the influence of the English government and of the Welsh Marcher lords steadily waned; but Gerald was in the service of the English. On the other hand he felt all the time, if his later testimony can be accepted, that he was kept back from the preferment due to him by his Welsh connexions. King Henry and the later government in England would not do anything to help a kinsman of the great Rhys, however worthy and loyal he was. It is hard to see where the truth lay. For Gerald himself tells us that he was offered two Welsh bishoprics, Bangor and Llandaff. Does this mean that he would only take St. David's or does it not mean that at this time his main preoccupations and ambitions were not Welsh at all, that he did not wish to be put away in a corner? And later, when hope of real eminence had gone, did his thoughts turn to St. David's again, and all his latent patriotism awake at the thought that he might rule his native land as an archbishop?

Gerald, you must remember, was not a saint and was too much concerned with the interests of every day to be an idealist or a dreamer. It would be foolish to look for consistency in such a man, and even in Wales at this time patriotism was not a burning consistent flame, least of all in the perplexing south, with its mixture of races, its family feuds, and political incoherence. When Gerald boasted of being a Welshman, or complained that his Welsh ancestry barred his way to preferment, he meant that his dignified Norman-Welsh origin put him above the ordinary man, and quite apart from the Englishman, whom he despised. And he also meant that he was regarded as peculiar and, perhaps, dangerous. Such a man, in a strange court with his way to make, is almost forced into opportunism, and the wonder is that Gerald was as consistent as he was. He responded very easily to his surroundings, yet he was always himself. He threw himself wholly into the duty or interest of the moment, yet he was always the detached critic of everything and everybody but himself. He had the detachment of the aristocrat and also of the *littérateur*, and this quality, and also his freedom of speech, his incisive tongue and vanity, while they doubtless prevented advancement, always made him a centre of interest. He got his full share of attention, and while men laughed at him or played up to him, they could not fail to respect him nor afford to disregard him. In short, he was a conspicuous person, though not so important as he imagined himself to be.

During these years he moved freely among the great. Some of the most interesting of his recollections are the records of conversations with the famous justiciar, Ranulf Glanvil, who chatted to him about politics. One memorable talk was on the causes of the growing weakness in the Angevin empire, of the steady development of French power. Gerald was increasingly impressed by the French; and in later life his sympathies were with the King of France rather than with the King of England. He was intimate, so far as was possible, with Henry II and his sons, but he was never captivated or overwhelmed by them; his heroes were Philip Augustus of France and his son Louis. This change of mind began during the last years of Henry, when Gerald was in touch with all parties during the dreadful quarrels between the old king and his sons, and his story is to be found in the late treatise on the education of a prince, in reality a desultory history of the West, based largely upon Hugh of Fleury, and passing into recollections of his own time. The book is an important authority for the history of Henry II, but its interest to the biographer of Gerald lies in its attitude to the French king. He was in Paris, a young student of twenty, when the future Philip Augustus was born and recalls how he went out into the streets and saw excited women rushing about with torches and prophesying a great future for the child. He had been told how, in his early days as king, when he was fifteen or sixteen years of age, Philip was one day seen to be lost in thought, idly twisting a stick with his fingers. One of the barons said he would give a good horse to know what the king was thinking about; another dared to ask him, and learned that Philip was wondering whether God would ever restore the kingdom to the greatness it had in the days of Charlemagne. The treatise, if dedicated at all, would, says Gerald in his preface, be dedicated to the young Louis, Philip's son. The preface must, I think, have been written while Louis was in England, seeking to conquer the realm in alliance with the rebellious barons (1216–17). And there is some evidence which suggests that Gerald was possibly in London while it was occupied by the French prince. Certainly in his eyes the Angevin kings deserved all their trouble and suffering.

King Henry II especially paid the penalty of his sins, his scandalous life, and his refusal to abide by the lesson taught by the death of St. Thomas of Canterbury. Gerald's interest in St. Thomas may best be described as that of an ecclesiastical man of the world, by which term I mean something different from a worldly ecclesiastic. He is the well-informed churchman, acquainted with the canon law and versed in ecclesiastical administration, who thought that Thomas was in the right and had behaved admirably. He had upheld the claim of the *sacerdotium* against *insular* tyranny (viii. 71–2). Gerald shows very little passion, takes the unity of the church for granted, and is mainly concerned to point out what fools the other people were and how badly Thomas's successors let the cause down. He quotes with some appreciation the remark of Richard of Ilchester, Bishop of Winchester (1174–88), one of the most distinguished administrators of his day, who had as a royal minister been opposed to St. Thomas. 'We were much deceived in that man. He was very different inside from his external appearance of display.' Some one observed: 'It is very remarkable that the church has not been able to secure a single one of the principles for which the martyr fell.' The bishop, more practised in affairs than in letters, replied, 'So far as he was able, the martyr secured everything. If his successor had had a tenth part of his goodness and honesty, the church would not have lost one of those principles.' Gerald was not an indiscriminate champion of these principles. He was a man of his day, and did his work under the conditions which he found, but in general Gerald was on the side of St. Thomas. Every ecclesiastic engaged in a conflict for rights could now feel that he had a great example; and we can see from the allusions to the martyr, scattered about Gerald's writings, how spontaneous and universal the interest in him was. When Gerald came back from Paris in 1180 he passed through Canterbury and visited the shrine. He tells how he and his companions came into an ecclesiastical council at Southwark *cum signaculis B. Thome a collo suspensis*, a reference to the thin, flat, purse-like little bottles of lead or pewter, in which pilgrims to the shrine carried away a tiny drop of the martyr's blood mixed with water (i. 55). Thirty years later on one of his journeys to Rome he heard an old friend of St. Thomas, John, Archbishop of Lyons, tell at Clairvaux of King Henry's indignant remark when Thomas insisted on giving up the chancellorship—'If an Archbishop of Mainz or Cologne can be the emperor's chancellor, why should an Archbishop of Canterbury refuse to be chancellor to the King of England?' (*Invect.*, ed. Davies, 97). Elsewhere he draws a pleasant picture of Thomas in exile at Pontigny, how when tired of study he would wander about from one of his companions to another, asking what they were reading. He gave currency—too maliciously, I think—to the story that one of the murderers had asserted the king's full connivance: Henry had not uttered wild unreflecting words, he had deliberately ordered the deed. He shows us the archbishop looking out of a window into the night, on the eve of his martyrdom, and asking whether he could reach the coast by daybreak, and then deciding to see his ordeal through, and he tells how, when the murderers came after

their crime to the archbishop's house at Malling, and leav
their cloaks and weapons on the heavy dining-table,
round the fire, the great table suddenly heaved and cast
unholy burden on the floor.

I come to Gerald of Wales as a man of letters. Ap
from some Latin poems, his first works were books
Ireland, the fruits of his visits (1183–6). Every one
heard the story, told by himself, of his triumph at Oxf
—how, on his return from Ireland, he came to Oxfo
gathered the learned clerks and others together, feas
them and read his 'Topography' to them. It was a curi
exhibition: a mixture of Celtic practice and literary sop
stication. The 'Topography' certainly had a good recepti
Archbishop Baldwin was so struck by it that he wan
Gerald not only to preach the crusade but also to go
the crusade as its historiographer. The books on Wales
lowed. The *Descriptio Kambriae*, so nearly lost, and
outcome of much labour, was finished at Lincoln, af
Gerald's withdrawal from court. It is a more sympathe
and better informed book, as one would expect, than
'Topography of Ireland'. As I said at the beginning of
lecture, these works have given Gerald his place in histo
They were his special contribution to the encyclopaedi
information which the wonderful twelfth century produ
—that mass of learning which included the scientific w
and travels of Adelard of Bath, the geography of the Ara
scholar Edrisi, the translations of the Koran, the theologi
method of Abelard and Peter the Lombard, the extens
translations from Greek and Arabic, of Aristotle and Gre
scientists. Gerald was for the most part oblivious to t
renaissance. He had heard vaguely that a number of boo
ascribed to Aristotle had been discovered at Toledo, a
he refers to a commentary upon the *De Anima*, but he h
no systematic knowledge of the new learning. He w
comed the ban imposed upon the study of the new Aristo
at Paris in 1210. He was apparently unaware of the devel
ment in mathematical science; but he was very sensit
to prevalent fashions of thought, and he had doubtl
caught something of the spirit of the new age. I do
know if he had read much of contemporary English histo

such as the important investigations of William of Malmesbury, but he was interested in the growth of Arthurian lore, and in one of his books tells the story of the discovery of King Arthur's body at Glastonbury. A faculty for gossipy, vivacious description of peoples and customs, an uncritical historical sense, an interest in philological speculations of quite an arbitrary kind—these were his qualities as a historian and they found their best expression in his books on Wales and Ireland.

But Gerald during the years before his retirement to Lincoln had lived in a wider world than Wales or Ireland. Scattered throughout his writings—and he never hesitated to repeat himself and to copy passages from earlier works—are numerous anecdotes and recollections of the days when he moved among statesmen and in high ecclesiastical circles. He was also a scholar and, absentee though he was, responsible for the administration of an archdeaconry. It was impossible for any writer who had studied in the schools of Paris to consider a problem of politics or church discipline uninfluenced by what he had heard there, and Gerald in particular was the last man to forget his Paris days. He had attended the lectures of the great Peter Comestor and frequently cites him. He had heard Peter the Chanter, or at least knew something of his writing, and Maurice the bishop, and many more. He liked to consider himself as one of the scholars of the day and he 'fancied himself' as a lecturer no less than a preacher. Naturally his administrative and practical interests drew him to the study of the law, and in addition to the Scriptures and the more accessible fathers, St. Jerome, St. Augustine, and so on, the great text-books of canon law—Burchard, Gratian, and compilations of papal decretals—were obviously familiar to him. One of the most delightful specimens of his naïve self-glorification is the account of his lectures on canon law during his second period of study in Paris (1177–80). When he began to lecture on the decretals, the crowd of doctors and students was so great that the largest school could scarce contain it. He treated his scientific theme with such beauty and colour of diction, such apt quotations, that the more learned his hearers were, the better they

were pleased. Such sweetness and grace of speech dı
away tedium, and the students rivalled each other in
eagerness with which they took down all he said, word
word. One highborn and intelligent canon of Paris as
Gerald privately how long he had studied civil and ca
law at Bologna, and when Gerald informed him that he
never been at Bologna, inquired where he had stud
Gerald replied that he had studied at Paris only for tł
years, and the canon departed in amazement. After bre
fast Gerald visited his own master and had the gratifica
of hearing him say, 'Your splendid utterance to-day be
that great audience pleased me more than a hundred s
ling brief.' And Gerald adds, 'As Jerome says, the suc
of his pupils is a teacher's glory.'

With however much salt we season this narrative, tł
is no doubt that Gerald's legal studies were of much ser
to him, both in his writings on the Church and in his
at Rome. One of these books—in some ways the best
ever wrote—was written at Lincoln: the *Gemma Ecclesias.*
Of this jewel Gerald says that he took it to Rome with
and presented it with other writings of his to the great p
Innocent III. The Pope kept the books by his bedside
a month, until he was persuaded to allow the cardinals
take them away to read—all except the Jewel—with
he would not part. The book was not widely circulat
but it was written primarily for the clergy of Gera
Welsh archdeaconry, and for this reason, he says, its st
is simple and unadorned. He had put together use
information—by way of precept and example—from m
authors, as a guide to the clergy in the discharge of tł
duties. He had dealt with the problems which he usec
discuss with them when he was living among them. A m
lively work on pastoral theology can never have been w
ten. It deals mainly with two matters—the eucharist
the morality of the clergy. The treatment is practical rat
than doctrinal, the problems those difficulties of every
which a clergyman has to face and are none the less d
culties because many of them are trivial. The book
professional, not popular, and we can realize from it h
the principles of the canon law and the doctrines of

Church fared in the test of experience in the twelfth century. We should remember that in those days many things which seem to us, as we look back through the centuries, to have been fundamental in the life of the Church were still new or awaiting more precise definition. Men were discussing them very much as they discuss to-day the issues raised by 'modernism' or by the proposed revision of the Prayer Book; they were discussed in the schools, and were finding somewhat puzzled or unwilling acceptance in the parishes. Gerald deals with the celibacy of the clergy, for example, with what at first sight strikes the reader as astonishing freedom. He says that he remembered a remark made by the great Paris teacher, Peter Comestor, to the effect that the greatest mistake ever made by the Church was its decision to impose clerical celibacy, and Gerald is clearly disposed to agree with his old master. Another feature of the book is common to all Gerald's writings—he can never resist a good story. One feels, indeed, that he would make a point in order to bring in a story rather than use a story to illustrate his point. It was rather unwise of him, an archdeacon, to go out of his way to attack the bishop's officials (the official, I should say, was the chief administrative and judicial officer in a diocese), but he had to tell the story of the clerk who was driven to blaspheme by losing all his money at dice. The clerk begged to know how best he could show his feeling about the Almighty by doing what was most abominable in His sight; and a friend advised him to become a bishop's official.

There are many stories, however, in the Jewel which illustrate in a very touching and wistful way the struggle between the pagan and the holy, or between reason and faith in a man. One of them is about an Englishman whom Gerald had seen in his Paris days, a master Richard (Albericanus) who had lectured with great success upon the eucharist, and by his self-discipline and austerities and almsgiving had striven in all ways to live a holy life; but on his death-bed he turned his face away from the body of Christ, because he had never been able to believe in his heart and had incurred the judgement of God. I cannot forbear to give another story, for it can never be told too often. A priest in the diocese of Worcester had been kept awake at night by the villagers singing and dancing about his house and in the churchyard. We can imagine the scene: a merry-making on a saint's day, the sound of voices in chorus through a summer night, perhaps the flicker of torchlight and shadows on the good man's wall. He rose in the morning to say mass, but when he began the salutation, *Dominus vobiscum*, he found himself, to his confusion, reciting in a loud voice the refrain of the love song which still rang in his ears—'Swete lamman dhin are'—'sweet mistress, thine aid' (ii. 120).

I must say very little about the third period of Gerald's life, covered by the reign of John and the early years of Henry III's minority. Gerald was about fifty-two years of age when he was elected a second time the bishop of St. David's, and a second time he was disappointed. He had accepted the offer of the canons with hesitation, but he would not give in again. Times had changed since 1176. Not only was Gerald no longer bound to the court, but the spirit of the Church was more assured, and a great man was on the papal throne. The adversary was not the new king, for John had been willing to accept him, but the redoubtable Hubert Walter, Archbishop of Canterbury, and for this very reason the issue was badly chosen, for Gerald was not able to say that he was fighting against secular interference. He could only maintain the right of the canons of St. David's to choose whom they willed by denying the archiepiscopal authority in Wales: and as events showed he had no chance of winning papal support for this position. However, he was determined. He disliked Hubert Walter, and in his advancing years his thoughts settled again upon his home and family. He went over to Ireland to discuss the position with his numerous relatives there and then set off for Rome. The story of the appeal, which lasted four years, and involved three distinct journeys to the papal court—so that the vigorous old fellow crossed the Alps six times—is told with a wealth of discourse in the last book of his 'Autobiography' and the six parts of the book incorrectly entitled the 'Invectives'. Documents were discovered in the archives of St. David's, and by Gerald himself (to his immense pride) in the papal registers at Rome. Pope Innocent was obviously attracted by the archdeacon. He liked his courage and vivacity, and the ingenuity with which he met the archbishop's arguments and faced his proctors. He wrote about him to the archbishop in a friendly way and begged that everything possible should be done to respect his feelings. But he could not give his countenance to the historical claim of St. David's to be the mother church of an independent province. A settlement was ultimately reached. Gerald of course did not become bishop and was formally reconciled to Hubert Walter. In his *Retractationes*, written after the manner of St. Augustine's, he withdrew his more outrageous charges against him. On the other hand the bishops of St. David's were not to be required in future to make a definite oath of obedience to their metropolitan.

Gerald lost nothing by his defeat. His English preferments and revenues were probably increased, and the king was friendly. He was able to maintain and add to his self-esteem. He had fought a good fight, and laid the foundations for success, he hoped, to be won by others in the future. Yet I fancy that he never recovered from the effects of these years. He could not forgive the canons of St. David's who had deserted and betrayed him; and St. David's meant a great deal to him. He lived for another fifteen or sixteen years, but gradually we lose sight of him. His later books—the *Speculum Ecclesiae* and the *De instructione principum* though very amusing and interesting, are not his best. They are informed by prejudice and violence unusual even in him. The one is mainly a diatribe against the monastic orders, the Cluniac especially and later the Cistercian. Gerald had suffered from monks, for all his successful rivals at St. David's were monks, and he was always opposed to monastic chapters in cathedrals and to the promotion of monks to bishoprics; but his unbalanced diatribe seems to be due to more than this. He had been the close friend of Cistercians in the past, and had written the life of that great monk, Carthusian it is true, St. Hugh of Lincoln. The other book shows that he had broken away from his old moorings in England, and yet he had nowhere else to go. Hence I will say no more on these works but call attention to a feature of his controversy with Hubert Walter.

The archbishop had begun his defence against Gerald by sending a rather unwise personal attack upon him to Rome. The pope invited him to reply, and the reply—the real *invectionis libellus*—is given in the first part of his book about the case. Hubert and his agents had ventured to reflect upon Gerald's Latinity. They could not have done worse, though they rightly guessed, no doubt, that they could not annoy him more. Gerald had very definite views about Latinity. Like his contemporaries John of Salisbury and Peter of Blois, he wrote with bitter sarcasm about the young men of his day, who rushed on to engage in fashionable speculations and disputes before they had learned their grammar. And he also believed very strongly in the value of a literate clergy and a learned episcopate. He particularly objected to the practice, so common in England, of electing as bishops clerks who had got their experience in the exchequer and the royal service. This reprehensible practice was one of the reasons why chapters should be allowed to elect canonically without interference. And here was an archbishop, who had no learning, and had spent his life among financial agents, daring to sneer at his, Gerald's, Latin, the Latin of a gentleman and a scholar. Gerald went back to one of his own books, the *Gemma*, for his retort and improved upon it. In the *Gemma* he had given many examples of the bad Latinity, the grammatical blunders and the appalling ignorance of the clergy. There was the priest who said that St. Barnabas was a good and holy man, though he was a robber, and quoted in support of this last statement, 'Now Barabbas was a robber'; and the priest who explained the meaning of the feast of St. John before the Latin Gate (*ante portam Latinam*) by the assertion that 'this St. John was the first man who brought the Latin tongue into England'. And there was even an archbishop who made incredible errors. Now this archbishop was Archbishop Hubert Walter, and in his address to the Pope during the suit at Rome, Gerald did not hesitate to say so. 'Oh, if you could only hear the beast bellowing out his words. You would hear tropes and figures which even Donatus in his *Barbarismus* and Priscian himself do not mention. He is especially good at putting the accusative for the nominative; and how often he mixes up his numbers and genders.' Gerald proceeds to give examples, the third and last of which is as follows: 'On one occasion Richard, King of the English, used the Latin phrase "Volumus quod istud fiat coram nobis", and the archbishop, who was standing by him with many other important people, wishing to correct the king, said, "Coram nos, coram nos, my lord!" The king looked towards that learned and witty man, Hugh, Bishop of Coventry, who said, "Stick to your own grammar, my lord, it is better", and so convulsed the assembly.'

Gerald, I said, is known to us only by his writings—and these show us that he is well worth knowing. It is equally true that we can only appreciate his writings to the full if we know something of the times in which he wrote, for he is by no means a reliable guide, and he never troubled to speak of things in which he was not interested or concerned. We should never know from him that the reign of Henry II is one of the most splendid periods in English history. And how gladly would one have had, in addition to his description of Wales, a description of Paris, with its schools and teachers, of Henry's court, of the living instead of the dead Rome, of Lincoln and St. Hugh's new cathedral. Medieval writers, and especially writers like Gerald, did not consider that the life about them would pass away. They lived in the present. And few of them lived so intensely as Gerald of Wales. He had, I suppose, an ineffectual, in some ways a disappointing life. He was often very irritable and touchy and unfair. But he was essentially a happy man, attractive to us by his faults even more than by his merits. He enjoyed as much as he could in life, and if he could not enjoy some of it, he took his revenge later and enjoyed writing about it.

VII

STEPHEN LANGTON[1]

THE seven-hundredth anniversary of Stephen Langton's death might easily have passed unnoticed. He was a great archbishop, but his personality does not leave a clear-cut impression on our minds. Yet, when once expressed, the thought of this celebration must have struck all of us as happy and appropriate, stirring within us feelings of cordial, if vague, satisfaction, reviving within us a sense of intimacy with the past, indefinable, perhaps elusive, yet undeniably sincere, as though some long-forgotten memory had begun to work. Why should we feel like this about a man of whom we know so little?

Our first thought, I suppose, is that Stephen was an Englishman. He was the tenth archbishop of Canterbury after the Norman Conquest, and the first great English ecclesiastic in the primacy since the days of Dunstan. His two immediate predecessors, Baldwin and Hubert Walter, may be described as Englishmen; the others, from Lanfranc onwards, were Italians or Normans. Neither Baldwin nor Hubert Walter was a great archbishop, although the one was a good and worthy man, the other a great statesman. Stephen was a good man, a statesman, and also a great archbishop.

When he died, 9 July 1228, seven hundred years ago, he was probably between seventy and seventy-five years of age.[2] Since his boyhood he had, until ten years before, hardly been in England. He was here for two years after the quarrel between King John and the Church (the years of the Charter, 1213–15), then from 1218, for ten years as archbishop. He had come to manhood, to maturity, and to fame as a master in Paris; he had been called to the papal court as a cardinal and, like other Englishmen, might

[1] An oration delivered in the Chapter House, Canterbury, on the occasion of the seventh centenary of Stephen Langton's death (July 1928).

[2] In *Stephen Langton* (Oxford, 1928), p. 8, I suggested that the archbishop was born about 1165. There is reason to think that he may have been born about ten years earlier.

well have spent the last part of his life attached to the Curia, an ecclesiastical statesman at head-quarters. An accident—so it must have seemed—made him archbishop of Canterbury in 1206. Then came seven weary years of strife, argument, anxiety, relieved by long quiet days of study and meditation in the Cistercian abbey of Pontigny, the refuge of St. Thomas of Canterbury before him, of St. Edmund of Canterbury after him. In 1213 a prospect of peace and reconciliation was opened in England by the submission of the king, but the task of restoration was more wearisome, more anxious, than the period of waiting. Stephen was found to be a man of independent outlook, no wary go-between, but a real English prelate, troublesome to king and pope alike. He was suspended from his duties and was under a cloud for nearly three years, from the late summer of 1215 till the spring of 1218. He was well over sixty before he began his unquestioned rule as head of the Church in England and chief adviser to the boy king. He outlived Henry III's minority a little more than a year. The curious tomb which is said to mark his resting-place in this great church, half inside, half out, is not a bad symbol of his life: half in, half out of England; half a scholar, half an ecclesiastic; a friend of monks, yet a stalwart secular; a man drawn to the contemplative, yet choosing the active life; a cardinal convinced of the divine mission of the Church universal, a practical archbishop responsive to local needs and the value of local custom and local men; a champion of the liberties of all, yet a mainstay of unity and order.

Stephen Langton came of a Lincolnshire family. His father was an inconspicuous landholder, probably of English or Anglo-Danish stock—what in these days we call a gentleman farmer. A farm, the site of the old manor-house, to the west of the church at Langton-by-Wragby, is still surrounded by a moat which may have enclosed Stephen's home. Church and farm lie on the high ground some miles to the east of Lincoln; they look out over a spacious landscape of woodland and cornfield; the prospect, like the air, is fresh, clean, and untroubled. The memory of such a home can keep a young man steady, give a sanction, a value to integrity as part of the nature of things; it may retain such a hold over his loyalty that, however far away he may be, however long his absence, he always feels himself to be a stranger and foreigner until he returns to his native land. Stephen's political letters express a deep affection for his country; when he fears lest his duty to his God and to the Church should be weakened by his love for England, and repudiates the suggestion that long residence in Paris has made him indifferent, he writes with obvious sincerity.

Two popular schools of thought in this country about the Middle Ages, although they are in agreement about nothing else, agree in thinking that the thirteenth century is too remote from us to justify any sense of intimate sympathy. The one school would say that even the common-sense view of the plain man about the Middle Ages is a piece of idealism. Life then, if we revisited it, would be a horrible yet fascinating nightmare of filth and cruelty, shot through and through by glorious streaks of the sanity which few can ever reach, for it is the sanity which comes from a sense of perfect communion with God. The other school would say that the common-sense view of the plain man is almost sacrilegious. Life then was far too fresh, spontaneous, adventurous, devout, for our muddy comprehension, though shot through and through by evil things which have the brightness of Lucifer. There was, indeed, much in Langton's mind and experience, for there was much in the world about him, which would perplex us as strange and difficult. The stress differs from age to age. The rhythm of life, so to speak, changes, just as musical modes, familiar enough to one generation, sound odd to another generation. But the study of history is a vain pursuit if there is no continuity in life and thought. The objects for which men strive change, their moral values may change, but two things do not change, and these are mental coherence or the intelligible, and moral coherence, the quality always recognizable in character because it has health. We do not imagine that Aristotle's *Metaphysics* was really unintelligible to Aquinas, or that Vergil could not be appreciated by Dante. And, similarly, when we find men whose minds were steeped in the Scriptures and who lived in this land of ours, where for hundreds of years their fathers had lived before them, speaking words which we can translate and doing things which seem to us to be normal and sensible things to do, we are not justified in supposing that their health was not our health. That they saw some things more clearly than we see them, and that they did some things which we should not do, is a stimulus to our curiosity, not a barrier to our understanding.

But, we are told, national feeling, patriotism, sense of race, political tradition, did not exist or were quite different in those days: may not the feeling of intimacy with a man like Langton be a delusion—a consequence, not a cause, of our idea that we are bound by some spiritual kinship to the English of the days of Alfred or Dunstan or Chaucer? There is, indeed, a deep mystery here, but I doubt if the passage of time alone has created it. We may respect, yet be unable to appreciate our neighbours, and we are wont to say, in explanation of some forms of incompatibility, that certain people are not typically English. Or we recognize an English quality in a man who may be repellent to us on other grounds. However strange his speech, however puzzling his actions, he has something in common with us. Time does not run against this kind of Englishman.

By a not unnatural confusion, we are disposed to imagine that real Englishmen must always have thought as we think. Yet how few of us, if pressed, would agree with Sir Thomas More or with Oliver Cromwell, two of the most typical Englishmen of all time! Langton was not an Anglican clergyman in disguise; in fighting for the liberties of the Church, he was not fighting for the freedom of an independent Church of England. Perhaps what is common to all Englishmen of this type is that they give free rein to the English quality in them. Some men seem to distort this quality, or breathe an air of mystification into it, or even expel it. Our Englishry is compatible, for example, with wholehearted service to the cause of empire, or peace, or the Pope, but it is not compatible, until it is so affected, with some kinds of imperialism, pacifism, and ultra-montanism. We have modern parallels to Langton's difficulties.

Bishop Ullathorne described the behaviour of Manning as un-English ; but W. G. Ward gibed at the English Catholics as schismatic and anti-Papal. Manning said on the university question : 'The English national spirit is spreading among Catholics, and we shall have dangers.' Newman, on the other hand, wrote: 'I prefer English habits of belief and devotion to foreign, from the same causes and by the same right which justifies foreigners in prefering their own. In following those of my people, I show less singularity and create less disturbance than if I made a flourish with what is novel and exotic. And in this line of conduct I am but availing myself of the teaching which I fell in with on becoming a Catholic.'

Stephen Langton was English. He was even a typical Englishman, in the sense that he seems to speak, not so much for himself, as for something fundamental, a characteristic in the best Englishmen of all periods. Yet he was not an insular Englishman. He brought back and gave to England what he had learned on the continent. He is of the company of St. Wilfrid and St. Dunstan. We misunderstand the development of English society and institutions if we neglect the foreign influences which have persistently been at work in our country. There is something distinctive, a unique quality, in English history, but—until the eighteenth century at any rate—this quality is the result of the penetration of the West. A people which could survive the Norman Conquest and help to create an Anglo-Norman civilization could survive and also absorb anything. Stubborn persistency and receptiveness, not insularity, are the marks of the English throughout their history. They acquired early the habit of giving and taking, taking and giving. St. Boniface and Alcuin almost literally gave western Europe a new start, but they came from a land which had been fertilized by Gregory the Great and Theodore of Tarsus. In the twelfth and thirteenth centuries the process of taking and giving was so continuous that England, on the edge of the known world, was drawn into a cosmopolitan society. Langton's life falls in the middle of this period, which began with the Arabic scholars and the monastic theologians of the early twelfth century and ended with the brilliant group of Oxford men who passed to and fro between England and France in the early fourteenth century. He grew to manhood in the schools of Paris and, when he was suddenly promoted to the cardinalate in 1206, had become their most eminent teacher. His work as archbishop and statesman was as clearly connected with his academic and intellectual interests as was the work of Pecham and Laud, but he was a much bigger man than either of these.

Langton studied and taught in Paris at a most interesting time. The cathedral schools were famous, and these were the years of their transition to the corporation of masters which was to be the governing element in the future university. As happens in a modern university, the cathedral schools of the twelfth century acquired atmosphere—their fame depended upon the vigorous interests which were prevalent there. Thus Chartres had been the main centre of humanistic studies. In Paris the humanities, law, and medicine were taught, but theology was the dominating interest, and in Langton's time it was a practical, moral theology, closely linked with the careful, but by no means stereotyped, exegesis of the Scriptures. Many other tendencies were at work, but their effects had not yet been felt, or, if felt, had not seriously disturbed the influence of the great masters. The Paris of St. Thomas Aquinas was to grow out of the Paris of Stephen Langton, just as, to take a later illustration, the Oxford of Jowett and Green grew out of the Oxford of Dr. Pusey; but in Langton's classroom the new Aristotle and the systematic dialectic of the schoolmen had no place. Langton had gone through the usual course in arts. He could cite Priscian and Boethius, make a somewhat fumbling and perfunctory use of formal logic, and quote tags from Cicero and the poets. But his real strength lay in what, I suppose, is now called pastoral theology. To this term, however, we must give a wide, far-reaching extension. Langton's outlook was the reverse of parochial. He grew up in the tradition or society of men who, on a broad basis of biblical and patristic, also in some degree of legal studies, were wont to face the outstanding issues in theology, ethics, and discipline. Moreover, the masters in the great cathedral schools of Paris were not recluses, expounding as dogma a well-defined system which they could not touch and never had to administer. It is very doubtful if medieval scholars at any time would have been satisfied with or would have deserved this modern description of their function. Certainly, if applied to the half-century which includes the great Lateran Councils of 1179 and 1215, such an estimate of their position would be ludicrous. The ecclesiastical system was passing through the process of definition, and the masters took the lead in the discussions. Matters to which time and authority were to give all the prestige of unquestioned truth were still open, or had been settled so recently as still to be within the region of criticism. Gerald of Wales had heard Petrus Comestor deplore the imposition of celibacy upon the clergy as one of the most disastrous decisions ever made in the history of the Church.

Langton devoted himself in the main to the study of the Bible. He is said to have commented upon all the books of the Old and New Testaments, including, of course, the Apocrypha, which was distributed among the books of the Old Testament. Some of his commentaries have not survived, and none of them have been printed. To judge from the manuscript evidence, his most popular works were the commentaries upon the Pentateuch, the four books of Kings, and the Minor Prophets, the last of which is stated in some copies to have been compiled in the year 1203. In the course of this comprehensive task of exposition, Langton decided to revise the existing divisions of the various books of the Bible. His new arrangement was adopted in the standard or Paris text, and it has descended from the Paris Bible to modern times. So it came about that Langton is responsible for the chapters which we use. As references are made to the old division in the exposition of the first three books of the Pentateuch and of part of Numbers, and to the new division in the exposition of the latter part of Numbers, it would seem that Langton decided upon his arrangement while he was lecturing upon the Pentateuch. The commentary on the Minor Prophets also uses the old divisions, so that, if the date 1203 is correct, and is not, as is quite likely, the date of some later copy, we could attribute the new division to the last three years of Langton's teaching in Paris.[1]

The commentaries were based upon lectures. Originally they were oral expositions. We know from later evidence that Langton would call attention to wrong readings in the Biblical text, and that his hearers would then correct their copies. He may thus have had his share in the production of the Paris Bible, afterwards severely criticized by Roger Bacon as a casual and capricious form of the sacred text. Some writers have supposed that he had a knowledge of Hebrew, but—though here I speak without any authority—I think it more likely that his acquaintance with critical and philological matters was confined to the 'interpretations of Hebrew names' and other guides available to the scholar.[2] However this may be, his work upon the Scriptures is remarkable, not for scholarship or method, but for a strange mixture of shrewd common sense and a fanciful exuberance in the moral style of exposition. It is the work of a practical, clear-sighted man, who was also a famous preacher, concerned with everyday problems ; it is also the work of a man peculiarly sensitive to all the impressions, analogies, associations, however far-fetched or fantastic they might be, brought into his mind by the words of Scripture. The same qualities are found in his sermons, and, with less violence of contrast, in his most important writings, the general lectures or *questiones* on theological and moral subjects. One moment we hear the quiet, cool voice of the man of the world who sees things as they are : the next moment we are carried into that apparently chaotic region of fanciful lore which meets us in the bestiaries and encyclopaedias on the nature of things. In a word, Langton was a man of his time. The same apparent contrast meets us in Roger Bacon and in Albert the Great. In another form it runs riot in the English literature of the seventeenth century. It is impossible to the educated man of to-day because he instinctively reduces phenomena to the principles of development and species ; but it can still be found in the speech

[1] This argument is very tentative, and should not be accepted as more than a suggestion until more work has been done on his commentaries.

[2] Works of this kind are also attributed to him.

of unsophisticated peasants, and in less pleasant forms it is not unknown among the over-civilized.

We put barriers to our understanding of medieval thought if we imagine that because Langton and his colleagues had not our criteria for judgement, they were afflicted by any disorderliness of mind. The world, in their view, was made like that, full of a number of different things. The great fundamental principles of natural law—the things in which, as the guide of life, man has found well-being—were to be found in the Scriptures. What more natural, therefore, than that the texts of Holy Writ should point to all sorts of truths helpful to man in his perplexities, or, conversely, than that the teacher should see everywhere in these texts the divine enforcement of the lessons which he wished to drive home?

Let us glance at this English master, talking with his pupils in Paris about the Pentateuch and the Minor Prophets.[1] Many of us have been reading lately about the wandering scholars. Langton had no use for *them*. The Vulgate of Micah i. 13 reads: 'The tumult of a chariot hath astonished the inhabitants of Lachis; it is the beginning of sin to the daughter of Sion.' Lachis is the roving which is the beginning of sin to the monks and scholars who, when they should be engaged in study or contemplation, scour the streets and highways as vagabonds, paying no heed to the warning of Solomon: 'Look not about thee in the ways of the city.' The master has a responsibility for as well as towards his pupils. In the Jewish law we read (Exod. xxi. 35, 36), 'And if one man's ox hurt another, that he die, then they shall sell the live ox and divide the money of it; and the dead ox also shall they divide. Or if it be known that the ox hath used to push in time past, and his owner hath not kept him in, he shall surely pay ox for ox; and the dead shall be his own.' A master's quarrelsome pupil injures the pupil of another master. The two masters must combine together to do justice, dividing the price, each sympathizing with the injured, taking no side but behaving with charity. If, however, the first master was

[1] I am indebted for the passages which follow to B. Smalley, who has permitted me to select examples from her transcripts.

aware of his pupil's fault and had failed to correct him, he must strive hard for the restoration of the injured man to health and must be responsible for the whole penalty; *error discipuli culpa est magistri*. The interpretation, or, rather, the explanation of a biblical text, is frequently illustrated by some incident which the master has noted, or some tendency which perhaps he has had to check in himself. Thus the words of Hosea (ii. 12), 'I will lay waste his vine', suggest of all things lax behaviour in church. Langton corrects the text. The vines are not destroyed, but damaged, as when a man who goes habitually to church gradually loses his reverence. As though he were at home, his thoughts during Mass dwell entirely on his studies or his business. His vineyard is damaged. But there can be vainglory in church. Amos (vi. 5) rebukes those who 'chant to the sound of the viol and invent to themselves instruments of music like David'. This, says Langton, is against those who sing Alleluia to the organ at Mass, on the pretext of devotion, for the sake of vainglory; as though they claimed to have the devotion of David, who humbly sang with musical instruments before the ark.[1] We remember that the future archbishop belonged to an austere school. His senior colleague, Peter, the cantor of Notre-Dame, had been one of those who deplored the lavish scale and artistic luxury of the new cathedral. Langton was interested in music. He very possibly composed the sequence 'Veni, sancte spiritus,' while he was a canon of Notre-Dame and teaching in the schools. His objection to the use of the organ during the long-drawn-out singing of the Alleluia between the Epistle and the Gospel is very interesting. As many passages in the liturgical works of the period show, the singing of the Alleluia was regarded as full of devotional significance.[2] In future years his own

[1] Trinity College, Cambridge, MS. B. 2. 26, f. 90r, comment on Amos vi. 5: 'Hoc contra illos qui specie deuocionis causa inanis glorie organice [*sic*] alleluia decantant in missa, tanquam se dicant habere deuocionem dauid coram archa musicis instrumentis humiliter decantantis. Sed non sic impii non sic.' A similar passage appears in a commentary on Amos v. 23 (fo. 88v).

[2] See the texts collected by Léon Gauthier (*Œuvres poétiques d'Adam de Saint Victor*, ed. 3, Paris, 1894), pp. 281, 282; on the use of the organ, cf. p. 305. I owe these references to Mr. W. A. Pantin.

noble sequence was given a high place among the musical elaborations which developed out of it.

Langton looked much wider afield for his illustrations than to the occurrences of everyday life about him. He was concerned with the welfare of the Church as a whole, and especially with its wise administration by the prelates, and the recognition of its place in the world. He would denounce those who lessen the measures, 'making the ephod small' (Amos viii. 5). These are men who have received wisdom in large measure from God, but who do not mete it out again, seldom deigning to preach. Their sermons to the rich are elegant and polished, but to the poor they preach bad, useless sermons, as though they are dragged out of them. Such men 'sell the refuse of the wheat' (Amos viii. 6). There are certain men who are like Jonah, who had to undergo his experience in the whale's belly before he could preach to the Ninevites: before they sin they are unwilling to preach, but after being ensnared and then freed by grace, they willingly take the duty upon themselves. A comment upon Joel (i. 11), 'Howl, O ye winedressers, for the wheat and for the barley', bearing on this theme, goes to confirm the conclusions reached by the late Sir William Ashley in his lectures on 'The Bread of our Forefathers'. Wheat, as Jerome says, is more precious, but barley is more fruitful and useful. Is not wheat the doctrine or preaching given to clergy and barley the preaching to the laity? The latter is coarser, but more fruitful and useful than the former. The criticisms of the prelates are still more vigorous. Langton was in the fashion—he said little that was new—but he had a more direct, pointed, practical intention than most of his fellow critics. His observations are the words of an observant man of affairs, rather than the objurgations of the ill-balanced preacher. Prelates and men of letters rejoice at the death of an ecclesiastical dignitary, as the tribes of Judah rejoiced at the captivity of the ten; they hope for his office. Bishops are too inclined to seek pretexts for excommunicating priests, so that they may extort a palfrey or some such thing from them: they 'sanctify war' (Micah iii. 5). Several times, in his work on the Minor Prophets, Langton turns to the story of King Ahaziah, who fell down through a lattice in his upper chamber that was in Samaria (2 Kings i. 2). Samaria means 'custodia', and Ahaziah signifies a prelate. The lattice windows, through which but little light enters, signify pastoral care in which is the dimness of perplexity. 'Truly in our times very little or no light enters by them, and many prelates tumble out of the lattices.' Prelates should be like the nail that comes out of Judah, the Church (Zech. x. 4). Nails are fixed on high in the tabernacle, where they support and spread out the curtains above the floor: so prelates in the Church are fixed on high, that by perseverance in good living they may keep their people from earthliness, supporting them by their example, by teaching and, if need be, by the giving of alms, and spreading them to their improvement. Langton returns again and again to the force of example, and to the duty of sustaining and encouraging the weak. The Church is in battle array, martyrs in the van, the fighters against anti-Christ in the rear, a great useless rabble in the middle. So in his sermon on the translation of St. Thomas of Canterbury—his exemplar—he compares the translation to its new shrine of the saint's body to the illumination of the sun in the heavens. The monks who serve him, maintaining the rules of their order, are like the moon in her place, drawing light from the sun. And the saint is serviceable to the sinners of this world, for the sun when it has risen draws drops of the salt sea, to which sinners may rightly be compared, by reason both of the brevity and saltness of mortal life, and of the bitterness of their sins.[1]

To Langton, as to any good churchman of the reforming school, the subjection of the spiritual to the secular was anathema. He was not an extreme papalist. He would interpret and justify ecclesiastical claims, the necessity of unity, in the light of the moral obligations of the Church. He was a realist. Thus, after giving the view that the

[1] J. A. Giles, 'Vita S. Thomae', in *Patres Ecclesiae Anglicanae*, (Oxford, 1845), xxxvii, pp. 296, 297. The whole address fills pp. 269–97. I have previously accepted the view that it was delivered on the actual occasion of the translation, 7 July 1220, but I am now disposed to think, from internal evidence, that it was preached to a congregation of Canterbury monks on a later anniversary of this ceremony.

secular power depends upon the spiritual, as the moon receives light from the sun, he admits that the theory is open to question. The Church gives doctrine and faith; in that case, at all events, the parallel holds, but, in fact, the sun often suffers eclipse from the interposition of the moon. What angered Langton was the acquiescence of the clergy in an unworthy dependence upon secular lords. Princes are not wont to act like the King of Nineveh, who 'rose from his throne and laid his robe from him and covered him with sackcloth and sat in ashes' (Jonah iii. 6). They approach the priest with an air of disdain, not humiliating themselves at his feet, but sitting beside him as though they would dispute with him. Prelates who take personal advantage of these secular claims do the Church dishonour. Langton, in a long passage, draws out a parallel between such men and Amaziah, the high priest of Bethel, who 'sent to Jeroboam, King of Israel, saying, Amos has conspired against thee', and at the same time 'said unto Amos, O thou seer, go, flee thee away into the land of Judah, and there eat bread and prophesy there; but prophesy not again any more at Bethel; for it is the king's chapel, and it is the king's court' (Amos vii. 10, 12, 13).

'There are ecclesiastics who will not move from their table to hear the confession of a poor man on his deathbed, though they will go two leagues or more on a winter's night for a harlot or for gain. To cancel their sin, they will accuse a good preacher of insulting the King, and if their report is not believed, will try to get rid of him: "You teacher, who come from Paris, and threaten us with all your preaching, get out of my diocese, go back to Paris to your studies.... You do wrong to reprove the King, for this place is his and it is for him to choose the parsons of this church." Bad prelates, indeed, are wont to say that they act upon the authority of Emperor or King. If they are resisted, they scold, saying, "You are acting against the King or Emperor, for you despise his institutions." So they flatter princes, that what they have done may seem to have been done by the princes.'

If Langton had died as a master at Paris, these passages would have had their interest as criticisms of the life of his time: they have a more important significance as the revelation of the mind of a future cardinal and archbishop of Canterbury, who helped to shape events during a formative period. The commentaries, lectures, and sermons give us some idea of the principles which directed Langton's activities. They are very simple, direct, moral principles, naïve yet far-reaching. This was the man who rallied the magnates and judges of England to define the customs of English administrative life, the privileges of the various orders of society, the implications of the coronation oath; who tried to restore the Church in England to self-respect after the indignities and spoliation suffered during the Interdict, who asserted the customary rights of the English prelates even against the agents of the greatest of medieval popes; who afterwards supervised the reorganization of dioceses, and developed the provincial assembly or Convocation of Canterbury on a representative basis; and, finally, who used all the authority of the ecclesiastical arm to maintain the throne of the young king, Henry III. It is difficult, if not impossible, to discuss the significance of Langton's views without a careful examination of the nature of society seven hundred years ago. A point which strikes us at first as odd, naïve, even childish, may become full of meaning in the light of feudal custom or ecclesiastical discipline. But, running the risk of anachronism, I will conclude with a brief summary, expressed so far as possible in general and modern terms, of the archbishop's opinions. They have no claim to originality save the originality which always belongs to opinions firmly held by a man who is strong and clear-sighted enough to act upon them: but they may appear to be not altogether irrelevant to present problems and discontents.

All men are subject to the law of nature, whose precepts are revealed in the Scriptures. Every power is subject to it, so that neither pope nor kings can disregard it. Christ is the head of the Church, but the Pope is His mouthpiece, and only the event can show how far papal authority, deliberately expressed with the counsel and consent of his cardinals, can extend, for who resists him resists the ordinance of God. He is the exponent of the moral law, and when he has spoken his decree must be observed, though it may surprise us and be contrary to our own teaching. In other words, the judgement of the Church is not arbitrary. Just as it is the duty of teachers to discuss the bearing of the moral law, so it is the function of the authority, where necessary, to close an issue. The prince is in a different position. He also is subject to the law, both the law of the community, so far as it is in accordance with the law of nature, and this law of nature or moral law, but the princes of the Church, as the exponents of the latter, can declare that he has failed to observe it. In feudal terms, if a prince fails in his allegiance to God, his overlord, his subjects must recognize the higher claims of the overlord. They must not use their own discretion. They must obey even an unjust judgement if it is made in the King's court—that is to say, formally decreed by the King and his counsellors—but they need not obey an unjust command which has not this sanction. In modern terms, there is no absolute or state sovereignty. Secular government is part of the divine order, and has its own law subject to the moral law, but it is not the final judge of this moral law, any more than the executive is the judge of lawful custom. The phrase 'a state Church' would have been meaningless to Langton; but so also would have been the idea, so often expressed nowadays, that the Church has no responsibility in matters of state. All human activities are subject to God's ordinances. This, however we express it, is the main lesson which the modern can learn from the medieval world.

The responsibility of the Church, and especially of prelates, is all the greater because their privileges are great. Ambition is natural in a prince, but a sin in a prelate. The clergy, either singly or as corporations, have a proprietary right in the goods which they enjoy, but their trust is all the greater. They cannot isolate its use from the welfare of the community in which they live. If a prince is in real need in a just cause, they should help him freely, although he has no *right* to tax spiritual property. If the poor are in need, they must nourish them. Everything is a trust, and in many ways the laity have more claim than the clergy. There are some things which the clergy should not reveal to the laity, but it is a finer and more useful thing to minister to the laity, to spend oneself upon them, in preaching and visitation, than to occupy oneself with fellow clergy. At present the Church is largely a rabble, but we must hope and work.

The appointment of good prelates is vital. Everything turns on that. To appoint to a bishopric a recluse, a contemplative, who has his own proper vocation, is rarely wise. A prelate must be sagacious, experienced, learned if possible, and absolutely disinterested. He must not regard his diocese as a vested interest, protected by the power ot the world, but must give a welcome to all good teaching. (Langton, it may be remarked, had been in Rome when St. Francis was causing a stir, and had, like St. Dominic, preached against heresy in France. He welcomed the two mendicant orders when they sent their mission to England.) Nothing is too minute for the attention of a good prelate and priest, but some things are indifferent and many things are unknown or insoluble. Anything in conduct, as in ritual, which suggests vainglory and show is bad; so is idle wandering and fussiness. The teacher has the right to explore unsettled questions and the duty to discuss the minutiae of moral and pastoral theology. We must face things as they are and use our common sense, and not be afraid to say that we do not know. There is no room for pedantry. Obedience is due to authority: but conscience has its rights, for—as I understand Langton—a wise superior will explain why an order is given, and this gives the subordinate an opportunity, under certain circumstances, to exercise his judgement. Thus if a canon with no obligation to reside is studying in the schools, and is ordered to return by his bishop, he must return if the intention is to strengthen the chapter; but if the order is given in his own interest he has a right to assert his view. If Langton, as archbishop, acted in the spirit of his early teaching, he must have been an enlightened as well as a firm disciplinarian. As primate he thought that the constituted authorities should, so far as possible, be left to manage the affairs of the Church in England with the aid of the local clergy. He was always prepared to reason with the Pope, just as in the end he would, if he could not carry his point, obey. It was said during some recent discussions 'it was not inconceivable that the Sovereign Pontiff might allow that normally the local authority should work without his intervention'. In the thirteenth century the Pope intervened daily. Appeals to Rome were almost a matter of course. But, Langton believed, there was no need to send in legates and promote foreigners.

Langton is a vague figure; but one seems to see through the mist an austere, just, hard-working, very observant and understanding man. Full of curiosity, he never lost his balance. A good talker among his friends, a helpful, stimulating teacher. As a statesman and prelate, a man who went straight to the mark, yet took endless pains. Impatient of disorder and extravagance in conduct, he believed that every one had his place, and that self-surrender to duty was the way to peace, a rational cheerfulness in obedience the safeguard of a true inner freedom. He was one of those strong, humble souls who do not appeal to the imagination, though they win the respect, of men, because they have deliberately subdued the spirit of adventure in themselves, and directed all their energy to making the place they live in more orderly and efficient. That is one side of the archbishop. There is another side, less clear to us—the student who could lose himself so easily in the intricacies of fanciful speculation, the man who brooded over the problem of penitence, the priest who liked to think of crusaders and Templars and the contemplatives of the cloister, the ecclesiastic who could strike hard and fiercely when occasion arose. And, binding together both the clear-headed man of affairs and the self-imprisoned adventurer, was the power of conviction: the deliberate belief, denied the personal certainty of a mystical experience, in the futility of man unless he has thrown in his lot with God, the sense of the unfathomable in God and the reliance upon the consoling presence, the Spirit of God:

> In labore requies
> In aestu temperies
> In fletu solatium.
> Sine tuo numine
> Nihil est in homine
> Nihil est innoxium.

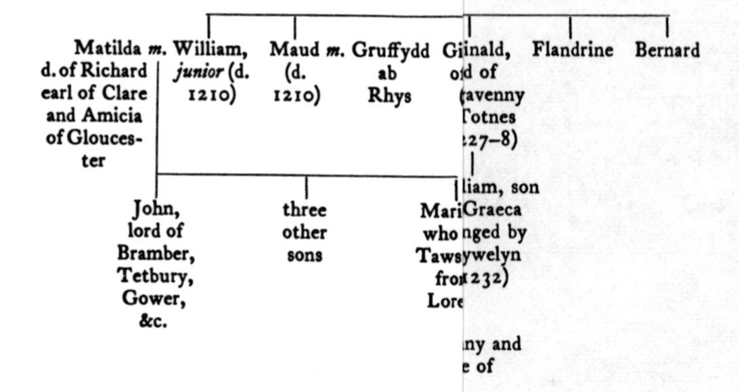
Matilda m. William, junior (d. 1210)
d. of Richard earl of Clare and Amicia of Gloucester
Maud m. Gruffydd ab Rhys (d. 1210)
Flandrine
Bernard
John, lord of Bramber, Tetbury, Gower, &c.
three other sons

VIII

LORETTA, COUNTESS OF LEICESTER

IN the Middle Ages old ladies did not dictate their reminiscences.[1] If some of them could have done so, we should know more about the times in which they lived than we can ever hope to learn from chronicles and records. Eleanor of Aquitaine, for example, who was over eighty when she died in 1204, could have told us much that we should like to know and never shall know. Denise of Anesty, who was twice widowed, in 1234 and 1255, and died in 1298, must have known a great deal about the inner history of the English baronage. And the subject of this essay, whose husband died in 1204, and who herself was alive when the battle of Evesham was fought, had memories which would have been very precious. Very few details of her long life are known to us, but what can be known of her is well worth telling, and, when considered in the light of other evidence, can be invested with some significance.

Loretta was one of the daughters of William of Briouze, first the friend, later the victim, of King John. She married the last earl of Leicester of the house of Beaumont. For nearly fifty years she was a recluse near Canterbury, where she protected the Franciscans after their first arrival in England. Towards the end of her life she was consulted by Simon de Montfort on a matter of state. Throughout her long and retired life she lived in the heart of things, as a girl and young wife and widow in Anglo-Norman society, as a middle-aged and aged woman near the shrine of St. Thomas. Her friends and relatives, whether lay or clerical, were to the fore in the political and religious life of England and Wales, of France and of Ireland. Yet to the chancery clerks she was a half-forgotten 'recluse of Hackington'.

[1] Since this sentence was written, Miss Hope Emily Allen has called attention to the newly discovered reminiscences of Margery Kempe of Lynn, written in the first half of the fifteenth century. Margery Kempe was an anchoress when she wrote the book (*The Times*, 27 December 1934).

I

Loretta's father, William of Briouze, was one of the most powerful barons in the Anglo-Norman state. His later life is part of the history of England, Wales, Ireland, and Normandy. He had inherited in the male line the lordships of Briouze and Couvert in Normandy, the rape of Bramber in Sussex, Builth and Radnor in the Welsh Marches. His grandfather Philip had married the heiress of Barnstaple and Totnes in Devon, and with some difficulty William established his right to these baronies. His father, also William, had made a still more important marriage, for his wife Bertha, surviving a long series of brothers, had brought him the great fiefs of her father Miles of Gloucester in the districts of Brecon and Upper Gwent. Our William was lord of Brecon and Abergavenny, of Hay, Pain's or Maud's Castle as well as of Builth and Radnor. To these King John added the rich peninsula of Gower in South Wales, and the honour of Limerick in Ireland. William succeeded his father about 1180, when his exploits, culminating in the slaughter of leading Welshmen at Abergavenny in 1176, had already made him very terrible to his neighbours. As his eldest son, William *junior*, was old enough in 1190 to have bought wardships and to have been in charge of royal castles, William was probably born about 1140 and had married some twenty years later. His wife was Maud or Matilda of St. Valéry, probably a daughter of Bernard of St. Valéry, and sister of the Thomas of St. Valéry who was prominent in the days of King John. William and his wife had sixteen children, ten sons and six daughters. In addition to William *junior*, Maud, Giles, who was consecrated bishop of Hereford on 24 June 1200, Margaret, Annora, Loretta and Reginald survived the perils of childhood.

As they grew up, four, if not five, of the children were married to the sons or daughters of Welsh or Marcher lords. Maud, named after her mother, was the eldest girl, and by 1189 was the wife of Gruffydd, the son and heir of the great 'lord Rhys', who in the later twelfth century dominated the politics of South Wales from his new stone castle at Aberteifi. William *junior* married a daughter of Richard, earl of Clare and Hertford, who, though not himself connected with the Welsh March, had close traditional interests which he had revived by his own marriage with Amicia of Gloucester. William *junior* thus became the nephew by marriage of Isabella, the first wife of King John. His eldest son, John, probably named after the future king, a friend of the family, was born on 6 October 1198. William *junior*, therefore, was married some time before the end of 1197. About the same time Reginald, the youngest surviving child, married Graeca, a daughter of the powerful counsellor and judge, William Brewer. William, the ill-fated son of Reginald and Graeca, was born before the end of the century. Graeca was dead before 1215, for in that year Reginald, now a violent foe of the king, sealed his alliance with Llywelyn ab Iorwerth, prince of Snowdonia, by a marriage with Llywelyn's daughter Gwladus Du. In the year 1200 Margaret of Briouze was married. Her father chose for her one of the great lords of the conquered Ireland, Walter Lacy, lord of Meath. The marriage was arranged during a brief visit of Walter to his extensive fiefs in Shropshire, Herefordshire, and Gloucestershire. He ruled these from Ludlow and Weobley. He also possessed rich fiefs in Normandy not so very far from Briouze. This alliance with a neighbour of the Welsh March was followed by another, for Annora, who was the twelfth child of William of Briouze, was married to Hugh, the heir of Roger Mortimer of Wigmore. I shall have occasion to speak of her later.

Loretta was married, I imagine, sometime after 1196. As she lived till 1266 and possibly later than that year, and as it would be unwise to suppose that she was much older than eighty years when she died, we can hardly date her birth earlier than 1180. She must have been a young girl when she married that tried warrior and statesman, Robert fitzParnel, earl of Leicester. Earl Robert in any case had not much time to think of marriage before 1196. The crusade with King Richard, the gallant defence of Rouen and Normandy during the king's captivity, then his own captivity in the hands of Philip Augustus, had given him no opportunity for domestic life. And during his half-dozen years of married life, he cannot have seen much of Loretta. He was with Richard and John, trying to save Normandy. Then in the early autumn of 1204 he died.

We are now in a position to form some idea of Loretta's early life. She grew up with a number of brothers and sisters in the midst of the strange society of South Wales. The elder children, William, Maud, and Giles, soon passed out of the family circle, nor would she see much of Reginald. Her companions would be Margaret and Annora, and especially that impressive woman, her mother. We cannot say whether she passed her early years in Bramber or in the lordships of Gwent and Brecon, and it is of course possible that she learned her psalter and did her needlework in some religious house. But she would see and hear a great deal of the life at Brecon and Abergavenny, and of her interesting relatives. We can learn much about the society of South Wales from that self-important, inquisitive, and attractive archdeacon, Gerald of Wales, a true son of the Marches, with his mixture of Norman and princely Welsh blood. In the days of the great Rhys, periods of fierce warfare and polite intercourse followed each other with bewildering rapidity. A seemingly internecine vendetta would be interrupted by the friendliest episodes, contests of song and arms, family alliances, giving and taking in marriage, ardent talk at festal gatherings about matters of church and state. Gerald was archdeacon of Brecon and had much admiration for the lord and lady of Brecon, especially for its lady, Maud of St. Valéry. Her husband William was a fine man, at once truly pious and ruthless in war; but in Gerald's eyes Maud was a paragon among women, one in a thousand, a good housewife and a shrewd, pungent critic of affairs. The archdeacon tells one story which illustrates the mind and spirit of the woman. It may be dated in the summer of 1200, when her son Giles had become bishop of Hereford. At that time the hot dispute between Gerald and archbishop Hubert about the bishopric of St. David's was a subject of much interest, frequently discussed when the great folk of South Wales gathered together. One day some of her companions were wondering why a man like Gerald should concern himself about so wretched and poor a diocese as St. David's. Maud burst into the talk and declared that, if she were a man and had the requisite learning, she would prefer St. David's to Hereford. The one gave opportunities for work and service, the other gave a life of ease and plenty, with small scope for a man of strength and energy: *virilitatis et vivacitatis pauca materia.* Maud clearly looked for spirit and a sense of adventure in her children, and was somewhat disappointed in Giles; or perhaps having used local influence to secure a good bishopric for her clerical son, she tactfully championed Gerald and his patriotic efforts on behalf of the exaltation to archiepiscopal rank of a bad one.

Virilitas and *vivacitas* in any case describe the character of the powerful woman who lingered long in Welsh memories as Moll Walbee and was believed to have rebuilt Hay castle in a night. Her outspoken tongue and vigorous insistence on her husband's interests were destined to bring her to a sad end. She came of a virile and vivacious family. Her brother,[1] Thomas of St. Valéry, who, in addition to his English lands in Oxfordshire, Berkshire, and elsewhere, ruled a rich fief in Ponthieu from his castle of Gamaches, was one of the most magnificent persons of the age, a mighty warrior, and a typical trimmer between conflicting loyalties when trimming was almost a necessary art in feudal lords who held lands on both sides of the Channel. Loretta would hear from her mother of Thomas and the other members of the family, of her grandfather Bernard, the *familiaris* of kings Henry II and Richard, who had died at Messina, of her uncle, another Bernard, who had gone to the Holy Land with King Richard and had died at Acre, of life in the pleasant land by the Somme, of St. Valéry itself, where the Conqueror had gathered his army for the invasion of England, of the family foundation at Godstow, handed over to King Henry, of Rosamund Clifford and her story.

After her marriage Loretta came into a different world.

[1] That Maud was closely connected with Bernard of St. Valéry and his son Thomas is certain, but genealogists do not agree about the exact relationship. She was obviously too old to be the daughter of Thomas and I have assumed that she was his sister and Bernard's daughter. Her marriage portion was probably the manors of Tetbury and Hampnett in Gloucestershire, which were held by the house of St. Valéry.

She left the castles of the March for Leicester, Hinckley, Mountsorrel, and Ware, quiet places in the Midlands, and Hungerford by the gentle waters of the Kennet. As a married woman she would see more of the royal court in England and Normandy. Her range of interests was greatly enlarged. Her father was a great man in the Welsh March, but his prominence as a royal counsellor began after Loretta's marriage. Earl Robert, on the contrary, had been at the centre of Anglo-Norman affairs throughout the reign of King Richard. A hero of the Crusade, and a man of loyalty and experience, he stood apart from the cliques of the court. His hereditary fiefs of Paci and Breteuil on the Norman March, and his family ties with the French baronage, gave him a standing which, while it did not shake his loyalty, compelled him to take a wide and serious view. One of his sisters, Amicia, had married the lord of Montfort in the Île de France and, when Loretta joined the family of Beaumont, was the wife of William des Barres, count of Rochefort, the most illustrious companion of King Philip Augustus and one of the greatest men of his age. In due course Loretta would feel the influence of that religious zeal which drove Amicia's son, Simon de Montfort, to lead the crusade against the Albigensians, and of those constructive forces which were rapidly making the French court the centre of western civilization. Her relations with her husband's mother, the famous Petronilla of Grantmesnil, would at first be still closer. Earl Robert was significantly known as Robert fitzParnel, a name which testifies to the strong personality of his mother, even though it were chosen to distinguish him from the Roberts who had preceded him. Unhappily, very little is known of Petronilla. One wonders if she told Loretta the story of the ring, how, after she and her husband, Robert III, were captured by the royal forces at Bury St. Edmunds during the rebellion of 1173, she threw a precious ring into a stream, before she was bound and carried off to prison.

II

When Loretta married she became, as any other wife became, a woman of property. She received a *maritagium* or marriage portion from her father, and at the church door her husband allotted her a dower, upon which she had the right to enter when he died.

Although the husband did homage to the donor for the *maritagium*, it remained as the portion of the wife unless she had children. Once a child was born the husband had in it an estate for life, and it passed later to the child and his heirs. If there were no children it ultimately would go back to the donor or his heirs, although the wife could enjoy it during her widowhood. Loretta, so far as we know, had no children; certainly no children survived their father; and so we find her in possession of her marriage portion after Earl Robert's death.

William of Briouze gave to Loretta and her husband the manor of Tawstock, near Barnstaple, together with thirteen knights' fees held of the honour of Barnstaple by Richard de Chartray. Tawstock was a large demesne manor which was obviously part of the honour of Barnstaple. Half of this honour was claimed by Oliver de Tracy. Circumstances were to favour the house of Tracy, not the house of Briouze, for when Oliver de Tracy died in 1211, William was dying in France, a refugee and a broken man. The Briouze family lost control of the honour of Barnstaple. Loretta, except for an interval of four years (1213–17), kept Tawstock, but this manor also came to the Tracys through the marriage of Henry Tracy with Loretta's niece, Maud or Mariotte, to whom Loretta gave it later.

In Normandy Loretta had Couvert, south of Bayeux, as part of her *maritagium*. The proof of this is a charter of King Philip Augustus, dated 1208, confirming extensive grants by Loretta to the monks of Lire, *de libero maritagio suo de Covert in Normannia*. Her father had, therefore, given the manor to Loretta free of service, and she had endowed the monks of Lire with lands, rents, &c., within it. When Philip Augustus conquered Normandy, the manor passed into his hands.

Loretta, after her husband's death, was allotted her dower, not a dowry which had already been defined, for Earl Robert does not appear to have made a precise allotment, but 100 librates of land. The process took some time, for it was involved in the discussions and arrangements regarding the succession to the earldom and honour of Leicester. At first some confusion was caused by an attempt, inspired by the old countess, Petronilla, to separate from the rest of the widespread honour the lands of the eleventh-century honour of Grandmesnil in England. Petronilla, the heiress of the Norman honour of Grandmesnil, regarded herself as the heiress of the English lands which had been merged a hundred years before in the honour of Leicester and had long ceased to have any connexion with the Norman house. The *curia regis* was at first prepared to admit Petronilla's claim and she made a fine of 3,000 marks with the king in order to have the ancient honour of Grandmesnil. There is some evidence that Loretta's dower was at first allotted to her from the lands of the Grandmesnil honour in Leicestershire. But the *curia*, which had wisely reserved the right to give further consideration to the matter, soon realized that the separation of this honour from the rest was wrong on historical grounds and unjust to the heirs of the earl of Leicester. Earl Robert's sisters Amicia (with her son, Simon de Montfort) and Margaret (with her husband, Saer de Quincy, lord of Leuchars in Fife and from 1207 earl of Winchester) were the heirs. Simon de Montfort and Saer de Quincy very properly laid claim to divide the whole inheritance. The honour of Grandmesnil, therefore, was taken back into the king's hands. It was probably soon after this that, with Saer de Quincy's aid, Loretta's dower was definitely allotted to her, not in Leicestershire, but in Hampshire and in the lands which formed part of the old sokes of Hungerford and Wimborne. In 1206 the commissioners appointed to divide the Leicester inheritance heard the parties and the evidence of juries. The division was made, saving the rights of the two countesses to their dowers, and Petronilla was compensated by the possession, in addition to her dower manors, of the rich fief of Ware in Hertfordshire.

As is well known, Simon de Montfort did not enjoy possession of his share, which carried with it the earldom, the stewardship and the lordship over the town of Leicester.

He was a foreigner and he did not pay his fine. A *custos* of the honour of Leicester was appointed, and the crown enjoyed the revenues until in 1239, by arrangement with his elder brother Amaury, the next Simon—the Simon de Montfort of English history—was allowed possession.

A widow's reasonable dower was normally one-third of her husband's lands. The husband may have endowed her with less, and at any rate until 1217, the third was regarded as a maximum, although before the Great Charter of 1217 a husband would sometimes say that if a specific dowry did not amount to a third, his widow should have enough in addition to bring the whole up to a third part of his total inheritance. The jurors of 1212 said that the earl of Leicester had definitely dowered Loretta with the manor of Kingston in Dorset (now Kingston Lacy, near Wimborne), but, as we have seen, King John and his advisers had at first fixed her dower at 100 librates of land in Leicestershire. In 1205, however, she got Kingston, also lands in Hungerford (Berkshire), and a large holding in the big Domesday manor of Chalton, in Hampshire, on the border of Sussex. In addition she had a part of the town of Blandford in Dorset. The total annual value of these lands was £140, well above the £100 fixed in 1205. The increase may explain the complaint that Saer de Quincy had been too generous at the expense of the heirs of the Leicester honour. Indeed, if we add the value of Loretta's marriage portion in Tawstock, she had a gross income of £184 a year. This must have corresponded fairly well to the value of Petronilla's dower lands, which, without Ware, the *solatium* added in 1205, had a gross value of £124. The gross value of the share of Simon de Montfort four or five years later was about £210. Saer de Quincy's share would be worth the same, and Loretta's dower of £140 was exactly one-third of the total, £420. In other words, she got one-fourth of the whole honour (£420 + £140), excluding Ware and Petronilla's dower. This neat result may be merely a coincidence, for we cannot be sure that all the data are available.

The gross total value of a fief was very different from the net value. Fixed charges, e.g. payments to religious houses, current expenses, loss of stock, and so on, had to be deducted, and in a bad year the deductions would be heavy. In 1207–8, for example, Loretta herself was in financial difficulties and had to borrow 100 marks from the royal Exchequer, to be repaid on 24 June and at Michaelmas 1208. An artificial and scattered estate could not be put into working order in a year, or even in two years. All the same Loretta had come off very well. She had very powerful friends at court. In addition to her father, now rapidly falling out of favour, there were the earl of Clare, William Brewer, and her cousin William Ferrers, earl of Derby. Saer de Quincy had been friendly, although at first Loretta seems to have been involved in legal difficulties both with him and with the old countess. In the spring of 1205 her attorneys in a plea of dower against Petronilla and Saer de Quincy were Richard of Combe and the cellarer of Lire, the Norman abbey with which the house of Beaumont had such close connexions.

III

Loretta was not long undisturbed in the possession of her lands. Already in 1207 the disputes between the king and her father had begun. In 1208 England fell under the Great Interdict. The dispute grew into a fierce quarrel with an excommunicated and implacable king. The anxiety and unrest caused by the interdict and the quarrel between John and Rome mingled with the hatreds which were kindled by a baronical schism. Loretta, so closely related to the chief royal victim among the laity and to one of the episcopal refugees among the clergy, could not hope to escape unharmed. She probably accompanied or followed her brother, the bishop of Hereford, into exile; and the events of these terrible years must have left in her mind, as they left in the minds of her sisters Margaret and Annora, ineffaceable memories.

The story of the quarrel between King John and William of Briouze and his wife has often been told, and need not be repeated here. I have given reasons elsewhere for thinking that a dispute about money—William's inability to pay the fine which he had promised for the possession of the honour of Limerick—was fanned into a vendetta by the indiscretions of Maud of St. Valéry, who revealed a secret then known to few, among them William of Briouze, the secret of the murder of Arthur of Brittany.[1] Maud would not give hostages to a man who had murdered his nephew. The outcome was John's campaign in Ireland against the offending pair and their son-in-law, Walter de Lacy, the flight and capture of Maud, the outlawry, after a last attempt at a settlement, of William of Briouze, and the starvation of Maud and her eldest son, William *junior*, in Windsor castle. The king, late in 1210, was driven to frenzy by the rumour that some of the barons had conspired to dethrone him and to offer the crown to Simon de Montfort, Loretta's nephew by marriage, who at this time was winning fame as a crusader against the Albigensians. The years 1209–11 saw the confiscation of lands, the seizure and imprisonment of suspects and their children, the flight of those who could escape. Loretta was but one of a group of *emigrés*, lay and clerical.

There is some indication that as early as November 1207 her security was in doubt, for at this time she entered into an agreement with the king that she would neither marry nor become a religious, that is to say, a nun or recluse, for a year from St. Andrew's Day. Her charter to this effect, attested by Walter Grey the chancellor, William Brewer, and others, was probably written on the day named, 30 November 1207. It was delivered into the royal chamber at Freemantle, the royal hunting lodge near Kings Clere, 9 December 1207. On 5 December the king, then at Freemantle, conceded to her the same liberties upon her lands as her husband had held, for a year from St. Andrew's Day. Now it is unlikely that Loretta had not previously enjoyed possession of her dower, which, as we have seen, was allotted in 1205; and, if she had been in possession, her agreement with the king, with its limitation of date, suggests that John wished to make sure of her. Relations between the king and her father were already strained.

[1] F. M. Powicke, *Loss of Normandy*, Appendix I, especially pp. 467–71. For the story as a whole, see Kate Norgate, *John Lackland*, p. 228 ; Orpen, *Ireland under the Normans*, ii. 236 *seqq.*

Moreover Loretta had already, it appears, begun to contemplate a life of religion as nun or anchoress, and John did not wish to see her escape from his control. She might be a valuable hostage. The danger of imprisonment was real enough. Loretta's sister Annora, the wife of Hugh Mortimer, was seized some time during these anxious years, and her sister Margaret no doubt fled to France with her husband Walter Lacy to escape a similar fate. After the murder of Maud and William *junior* in 1210, the latter's four boys, ranging in age from twelve years downwards, were seized, also Henry of St. Valéry, the brother of Maud and Thomas. All of these were later in the care of that cruel and unsavoury mercenary, Engelard of Cigogné, sheriff of Gloucester. They were probably immured in Bristol castle. Other victims were kept in Corfe, where Eleanor, the sister of Arthur of Brittany, was suffering the first stage in her long life as a prisoner.

Loretta was in a stronger position than these unhappy children, but it is not likely that she delayed her departure very long. Her lands were certainly in the king's hands in 1212, and may have been seized early in 1209, when Henry fitzCount, the natural son of Reginald, former earl of Cornwall, was given the custody of Totnes, her father's barony in south Devon. Henry fitzCount is found later in possession of some of her lands. If she did not go abroad it is hard to see how she could have lived in England, and strange to find no reference to her; whereas she was sure of a refuge in France. Hence I conclude that she followed her brother, Giles of Hereford, and was with her father when he died at Corbeil on 9 August 1211. There she would find Stephen Langton, the archbishop of Canterbury, who buried William of Briouze the next day at the abbey of St. Victor in Paris. The association with this great man and with the cultivated and deeply religious circle of her husband's relatives, the Montforts, must have intensified her spiritual life. Simon de Montfort, now far away in the south, was a man of fierce piety. He attended Mass daily, and was an example of that devotion to the Blessed Sacrament which, as St. Francis declared, was nowhere cultivated so seriously as in France. Loretta was about ten years younger than Simon, though she was his aunt by marriage. It is not too fanciful to suggest that she held in her arms his infant son, the future earl of Leicester and victor of Lewes, who was born about 1208. She would move in a family group composed of the great houses of Montfort, Montmorency, and Barres. She would see something of the monks and nuns of Vaux de Cernay, Haute-Bruyère, and Fontaine, the religious houses most affected by her friends. She would hear about the Crusade in the south, whose historian was a monk of Cernay, follow eagerly the phases of the dispute between Rome and King John, talk with learned and saintly men, and perhaps learn to venerate the martyr St. Thomas of Canterbury. She would see King Philip Augustus and his son Louis and Louis's young wife Blanche, *candida* in more senses than one, whose son, the future St. Louis, was born soon after her return to England. Nothing of all this can be proved, but it is the most likely picture that I can draw of Loretta's life during these years. At any rate it is more pleasant to think of her with Amicia and her family than as alone in an English castle or convent, or as dependent on the timid charity of Saer de Quincy or the aged Petronilla.

Her next appearance in the records is explicit enough. Towards the end of 1214 she made a deed, attested by Peter des Roches the bishop of Winchester, her brother the bishop of Hereford, William the Marshal, and others. In it she says that she had taken an oath upon the Gospels that she was not married and would not marry without the king's consent, and that she surrendered all claim to the proceeds of her lands during the period of their detention by the king.

Two facts stand out in this deed. The king and others had held and exploited her lands and the king did not know what Loretta had been doing, for if he had known, he would have required no assurance that she had not married again. The date, the Monday after St. Nicholas's day (5 December), was shortly after the great council in London at which the king, recently returned from his fruitless campaign in Poitou, had solemnly reaffirmed his promise to grant the freedom of ecclesiastical elections. It looks as though Loretta had come back to England during John's absence, and, with the help of the chief men of the realm, afterwards came to an arrangement with the king for the restoration of her lands. She seems to have held them through the civil war and for three or four years after the accession of Henry III. In the summer of 1219 she was preparing for retirement from the world, for on 20 June she made a grant of her dower lands for three years. On 19 February 1221 her name appeared upon a list of those tenants in chief who were allowed scutage for the service of their knights in the campaign against the count of Aumâle and his castle of Bytham. This must refer to the knights' fees on her *maritagium* of Tawstock. But the entry is crossed through, and, as this is the latest reference to her land, we may conclude that, when the list was tested, she was found to have given up possession. Hence she became a recluse about this time.

By this time her brothers and nephews had been restored to their inheritance. The bishop of Hereford and Reginald had joined the rebels in 1215 and co-operated with Llywelyn of Wales, but the bishop was reconciled to the king before he died in November of that year, and in 1216 Reginald had succeeded to the lands of his father. In January 1218 the four sons of William *junior* were released, and after a lawsuit with his uncle Reginald, John, the eldest, secured possession of Knap and Bramber, the seats of the Briouze honour in Sussex. Loretta's brothers-in-law, Walter Lacy and Hugh Mortimer, fought hard on King John's side and stood high in his favour. Before the king died, Margaret of Briouze, Walter's wife, stirred him to one inadequate and tardy act of reparation for the murder of her mother and brother at Windsor. At King's Lynn on 10 October 1216, just before his disastrous passage of the Wash and when he was already feeling ill, John granted to Margaret a piece of land in the forest of Acconbury, by Hereford. Her husband, then castellan of Hereford, was charged with the duty of selecting the site, and upon it Margaret was at liberty to found a nunnery for the souls of William her father, Matilda her mother, and William her brother. The medieval nunnery of Acconbury was for three centuries their silent memorial.

IV

Loretta became a recluse at Hackington, a mile to the north of Canterbury. She had doubtless fallen under the influence of Archbishop Langton and been stirred by the celebration in July 1220 when the body of St. Thomas was translated to its new shrine behind the high altar in Christ Church, Canterbury. This had been a European as much as an English event. She lived at Hackington for at least forty-five years and died there on 4 March, in 1266 or one of the next few years. She was buried in the church of St. Stephen, by which her cell may have been built.

Hackington, in 1221, had only recently ceased to take a very prominent part in the ecclesiastical life of Canterbury, for it was around a projected foundation of secular canons there that one of the most prolonged of the many controversies between the abbey of Christ Church, the cathedral church, and the archbishops had been fought. The scheme was now dead. Archbishop Stephen definitely repudiated the intention of his predecessors, and in 1227 allotted the church at Hackington as part of the endowment of the archdeaconry. It would fall to the archbishop in 1221 to approve the spot chosen by Loretta and to satisfy himself, before he gave permission to enter on her new life, that her means of livelihood were adequate.[1] When the day came, there would be a service conducted by the archbishop as diocesan or some authorized priest. According to a thirteenth-century *Ordo includendi famulam Dei* the simple office then comprised a Mass of requiem, during which, after the Gospel, the anchoress made her profession and was ceremonially clothed and veiled. After Mass the bishop's procession entered the reclusory, leaving the *includenda* outside, sprinkled it with holy water and blessed the water within. The bishop then came out and bade the *includenda* enter if she wished to enter. She entered, and part of the office for the dead was sung. In later times, but not according to

[1] Rotha Mary Clay, *The Hermits and Anchorites of England*, p. 91 and *passim*. I have also been greatly assisted in writing this and the following paragraph by Miss Dorothy Ellis, who kindly lent me some of her notes, including her transcript of the office in the Bainbridge Pontifical, Cambridge MS. Ff. VI. 1, f. 193. The date of the manuscript is fifteenth century, but Dr. Frere regards the *Ordo* as early.

this *Ordo*, the door was ceremonially locked and sealed with the bishop's seal.

The building in which Loretta lived would be of stone with a wooden roof or of wood alone. There was an inner room which was private and an outer room with a small window through which conversation with those visitors who were not privileged to enter might be made. Servants were allowed, and a great lady like Loretta would probably have two women, an elderly housekeeper who could provide for the small establishment, and a younger maid who was always kept at home, and did the rougher work. Loretta in addition had a man-servant, presumably a sort of agent and a man of business who could also act as a messenger. In 1235 he was a certain Robert Newton, and as he was exempted from the duty of serving on juries, he probably lived on some local tenement. Loretta would also be allowed to choose her confessor.

When a woman of high social position became a recluse —and in the thirteenth century many, if not most, recluses were such—careful arrangements were made for her future maintenance. Although little is known of Loretta's plans, we can get some idea of these arrangements from the scattered records of her sister Annora, who also was a recluse. Annora's husband, Hugh Mortimer, succeeded to his lands in 1214 and died in November 1227. In May 1215, some months after Annora's release from prison (October 1214), he recovered possession of her *maritagium*, the manors of Tetbury and Hampnett (near Northleach) in Gloucestershire. As she had no children, Hugh's heir, Ralph Mortimer, had no claim to her *maritagium*, which, on her retirement, fell back into the honour of the main Briouze line, represented by the heir of John of Briouze. The king, however, allowed her to reserve an income of 100 shillings in Charlton (probably Charlton Kings, near Cheltenham) and Cherrington (four miles north of Tetbury) which were parts of the manor of Tetbury and which her father, William of Briouze, gave to her 'as a marriage portion'. This permission was given on 28 September 1232 for her maintenance so long as she was a recluse. Here we have a recluse with an annual income of £5. She can be identified with

Annora, the recluse of Iffley, who frequently appears during the next few years as the recipient of the royal bounty. Iffley is not far from Osney, the old home of Annora's mother. Tetbury had been a St. Valéry manor, Annora bore a St. Valéry family name, and was a benefactor of what had been the family nunnery at Godstow. Her thoughts had been turned to Osney and Oxford and she decided to settle down by the Norman church at Iffley, a little way down the river Thames.

The story of Loretta's retirement is not so clear; but it is possible that when she handed over her dower lands in 1219 to the bishop of Winchester and Philip of Albini for three years, she intended to use the rent which accrued as the endowment of her anchorage. She must have had an income of some sort in order to pay her servants. Her maintenance was provided for, as was customary, by grants of food and firewood. One at least of her friends made an annual grant. Alice, the countess of Eu, the lady of Hastings and Tickhill, a very great lady indeed, made Loretta an annual allowance from her manor of Elham in Kent of two quarters of wheat—the food of gentlefolk—two quarters of barley, one of oats, and two sides of bacon. A recluse was expected to live an austere but not too ascetic a life. That very beautiful guide for recluses, the *Ancren Riwle*, a book which Loretta would know, did not encourage rigid asceticism, but moderation and everything which makes for a healthy and cheerful spirit, able to endure long, arduous service in the search for God.

Loretta was not a public figure, like the famous Christina, the recluse of Markyate, who in the days of King Stephen and King Henry II was the counsellor of prelates and magnates. But it is clear that she exercised a steady influence. As we shall see, she was an active friend to the Franciscans, and, in their spirit, she was always ready to take the needy and oppressed under her protection. Pilgrims to Canterbury may have sought her out, for she used her influence on behalf of persons from distant places as well as on behalf of her neighbours such as the poor people who could not afford to pay their share of the tallage levied at Canterbury. At her instance a woman who had given shelter to a fugitive from justice and been outlawed was pardoned, also a man from Shropshire who had killed another by misadventure. And she was willing on occasion to get a privilege for a neighbour, for example the prioress of the Benedictine nunnery of St. Sepulchre at Canterbury.

In the *Ancren Riwle* recluses are urged to love their windows as little as possible ; and we may be sure that Loretta was faithful to her rule and was no idle gossip. Yet it would be absurd to imagine that she did not have visitors and hear a good deal of what was going on. Nearly everybody of importance passed through Canterbury at one time or another, and many of her friends and kinsfolk in France and England would take the opportunity to go to see her. When, for example, Amaury de Montfort came with nine knights in 1235 to visit the shrine of St. Thomas, he is not likely to have forgotten the great-aunt who, in his boyhood, twenty-five years ago, had taken refuge in France. His brother Simon did not forget her. They had common friends in the followers of St. Francis, and it would be very good to have some record of the talk between Loretta and the Oxford Franciscan scholar, Adam Marsh, about the puzzling personality of the great earl of Leicester. Our most vivid picture of Loretta as a recluse is suggested by Earl Simon himself near the end of his life and hers. On 29 April 1265, three months before the battle of Evesham, King Henry wrote as follows to Loretta :

'The King to the recluse of Hackington greeting. Because you know better than others, so it is said, what rights and liberties appertain to the stewardship of England in regard to the earldom and honour of Leicester, we, wishing to be more fully certified on these matters by you, straitly require and command you forthwith to expound the said rights and liberties in the presence of our well beloved in Christ the abbot of St. Augustine's Canterbury and the prior of Christ Church in the same town, and to have them written down clearly and fully before them, and sent to us under the seals of the same abbot and prior.'

On the same day a mandate was sent to the two prelates enjoining them to wait upon Loretta on a day convenient to her.

The subject on which Earl Simon—for at this time King Henry acted under his dictation—asked for enlightenment is of some importance in medieval history, but unhappily Loretta's reply has not come down to us. In all probability it was not very helpful. But the royal letter shows that, even in 1265, Loretta was regarded as a woman of practical intelligence with a retentive memory. It must have stirred many early memories in her aged brain; first of her husband, as she tried to recall what he had done as steward, of his homecomings and his talk during their brief interrupted life together, of the places in which she had lived with him, then of all the other places familiar to her in her girlhood by the waters of the Usk and the Wye, of her father and mother and their vigorous life and sad death, of all her brothers and their children and grandchildren, of Margaret and her nuns at Acconbury, and Annora in her cell at Iffley. One of Margaret's granddaughters, over at Ludlow, had a young Frenchman as her husband, a brother of the lord of Joinville, the friend of the French king. And so before she turned to her prayers, she would be brought back to the perplexities of the present time, and to Earl Simon.

V

More than half of Loretta's long life was concerned, to the exclusion of every other interest, with religion. The time has not yet come to estimate the significance of the anchoress and anchorite in the history of medieval religious life, but, as the investigations of scholars proceed, it becomes clear that the old idea of anchorites and anchoresses as earnest eccentrics remote from the religious movements of their day is far from the truth. It would be more true to say that those who lived this solitary life helped to foster and enlarge the tendencies in contemporary thought and experience. In some ways they were the spiritual children of St. Anselm, in others careful and responsive converts to new forms of personal devotion to Jesus and the Virgin Mary. And we have recently been told how the literature of personal religion, at first Anglo-Norman as well as English, gradually became a means for the transmission and development of English prose.

We cannot estimate the measure of Loretta's share in the religious life of her time, a time when attempts to reorganize the English Church went side by side with a quick advance in religious expression, a time when recluses, many of them women of cultivated minds, were especially numerous in England. But she appears in the story at least twice.

Her first appearance in ecclesiastical history is the best-known episode in Loretta's life. It is mentioned by Eccleston in his history of the arrival of the Friars Minor in England (1224):

> 'Lord Simon Langton, archdeacon of Canterbury, lord Henry of Sandwich, and the noble countess the lady recluse of Hackington, were especially active in their behalf. The lady nourished them in all things, as a mother her sons, by winning for them in her wise way the good will of magnates and prelates by whom she was held in the highest regard.'

This passage is full of significance. We see Loretta, some three years after her reclusion, as a woman of influence, able to further the interests of a little group of strangers, whose unfamiliar speech and practices, exuberance, and entire dependence on charity repelled many women. When that joyous creature, Brother Salomon, whom the archbishop hailed as *de ordine apostolorum*, begged from his sister, she gave him bread with averted face and cursed the hour in which she had ever seen him. Loretta was able to anticipate and divert hostility of this kind, and to open a way throughout England for the disciples of St. Francis. As they prospered her own experience would be enlarged, and she would have the friendship of some of the most interesting men of her time. Moreover, she would hear about and be influenced by the life and work of St. Francis, a man of about her own age.

Loretta's next appearance in the religious literature of the thirteenth century has hitherto not been known. It comes in a collection of miracles of the Virgin, which since the seventeenth century has been in Vendôme. The manuscript, which contains several items, concludes with a collection of miracles, obviously based upon earlier works of the kind, but with additions which were made some time after 1235 in the Cistercian abbey of Vaux de Cernay. One of the additions begins:

'A recluse at Canterbury, who was formerly countess of Leicester, told me, the abbot of Vaux de Cernay [the following story], which she said that she had heard from trustworthy persons who vouched for its truth.'

The story which the recluse told the abbot was of the five joys of Mary, a theme which was often elaborated from a liturgical anthem *Gaude dei Genetrix* dating at least from the first part of the eleventh century. There were two women, great friends, and one of them, *longe religiosior* than the other, came to die. Her friend, standing by the bed-side, saw her smile five times, very brightly and happily. After her death she appeared to her friend and explained why she had smiled. She had been wont, during her life on earth, to divide the day into five parts, each devoted to a meditation on the Virgin. After rising, until prime she meditated on the joy of Mary in the annunciation, from prime to the third hour on her joy in the conception, from the third to nones on her joy in the resurrection of her Son, from nones to vespers on her joy in her Son's ascension, from vespers till she went to bed on the joy which she had in her Assumption. On her death-bed the Virgin appeared to her five times in succession, exactly as she had been wont to imagine her in her daily meditations.

There can be no doubt that the recluse of Canterbury was Loretta, and it is very probable that the abbot of Vaux de Cernay to whom she told this story was, as the editor of the manuscript suggests, Theobald of Marly, afterwards canonized, who was abbot between 1235 and 1247. Now Theobald was of the house of Montmorency, and related to Simon de Montfort's mother, that Alice of Montmorency who had married Simon the crusader, the nephew of Loretta's husband. Loretta had doubtless met him when he was a monk at Vaux de Cernay, the Cistercian house much favoured by the Montforts and the Montmorencys, and he had come to see her long afterwards when, as an old man, he perhaps made a pilgrimage to Canterbury. They talked about the religious life. The story obviously refers to two women familiar with the devotional tendencies of the time, and living the religious life as nuns or recluses. The life was inspired by the tradition of St. Anselm, John of Fécamp, and St. Bernard, and was lightened by that joy to which St. Francis and his disciples gave voice in their lauds.

INDEX